Form Design View Tool Bar

A B C D E F G   H   I   J K L M N O P Q R

A. Switch to Design view	B. Switch to Form view	C. Switch to Datasheet view
D. Print Preview	E. Display Properties window	F. Display Field List
G. Display Palette window	H. Font typeface	I. Font size
J. Bold	K. Italic	L. Underline
M. Left-align	N. Center	O. Right-align
P. General alignment	Q. Undo	R. Help

Form's Form and Datasheet View Tool Bar

A B C D E   F G H   I   J K

A. Switch to Design view	B. Switch to Form view	C. Switch to Datasheet view
D. Print Preview	E. Find	F. Edit Filter/Sort
G. Apply Filter/Sort	H. Remove Filter/Sort (Show All Records)	I. Display current field name
J. Undo	K. Help	

Macro Window Tool Bar

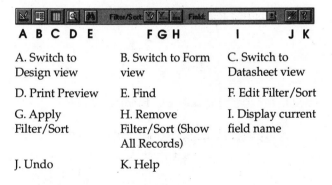

A B C D   E F

A. Show Macro Names column	B. Show Conditions column	C. Run
D. Single-Step Execution	E. Undo	F. Help

The SYBEX Instant Reference Series

Instant References are available on these topics:

Computer users are not all alike.
Neither are SYBEX books.

We know our customers have a variety of needs. They've told us so. And because we've listened, we've developed several distinct types of books to meet the needs of each of our customers. What are you looking for in computer help?

If you're looking for the basics, try the **ABC's** series. For a more visual approach, select full-color **Quick & Easy** books.

Running Start books are two books in one: a fast-paced tutorial, followed by a command reference.

Mastering and **Understanding** titles offer you a step-by-step introduction, plus an in-depth examination of intermediate-level features, to use as you progress.

Our **Up & Running** series is designed for computer-literate consumers who want a no-nonsense overview of new programs. Just 20 basic lessons, and you're on your way.

SYBEX **Encyclopedias**, **Desktop References**, and **A to Z** books provide a *comprehensive reference* and explanation of all of the commands, features, and functions of the subject software.

Sometimes a subject requires a special treatment that our standard series don't provide. So you'll find we have titles like **Advanced Techniques, Handbooks, Tips & Tricks,** and others that are specifically tailored to satisfy a unique need.

You'll find SYBEX publishes a variety of books on every popular software package. Looking for computer help? Help Yourself to SYBEX.

 For a complete catalog of our publications:

SYBEX Inc.
2021 Challenger Drive, Alameda, CA 94501
Tel: (510) 523-8233/(800) 227-2346 Telex: 336311
Fax: (510) 523-2373

 SYBEX is committed to using natural resources wisely to preserve and improve our environment. This is why we have been printing the text of books like this one on recycled paper since 1982.

This year our use of recycled paper will result in the saving of more than 15,300 trees. We will lower air pollution effluents by 54,000 pounds, save 6,300,000 gallons of water, and reduce landfill by 2,700 cubic yards.

In choosing a SYBEX book you are not only making a choice for the best in skills and information, you are also choosing to enhance the quality of life for all of us.

Microsoft® Access Instant Reference

James E. Powell

SYBEX ®

San Francisco • Paris • Düsseldorf • Soest

Acquisitions Editor: Dianne King
Developmental Editor: David Peal
Editor: Guy Hart-Davis
Technical Editor: Dan Tauber
Book Designer: Ingrid Owen
Production Artist: Alissa Feinberg
Screen Graphics: John Corrigan, Aldo Bermudez
Desktop Publishing Specialist: Thomas Goudie
Proofreader/Production Assistant: Arno Harris
Indexer: Ted Laux
Cover Designer: Archer Design
Screen reproductions produced with Collage Plus.
Collage Plus is a trademark of Inner Media Inc.
SYBEX is a registered trademark of SYBEX Inc.

TRADEMARKS: SYBEX has attempted throughout this book to
distinguish proprietary trademarks from descriptive terms by following the capitalization style used by the manufacturer.

SYBEX is not affiliated with any manufacturer.

Every effort has been made to supply complete and accurate information. However, SYBEX assumes no responsibility for its use,
nor for any infringement of the intellectual property rights of
third parties which would result from such use.

Copyright ©1993 SYBEX Inc., 2021 Challenger Drive, Alameda,
CA 94501. World rights reserved. No part of this publication may
be stored in a retrieval system, transmitted, or reproduced in any
way, including but not limited to photocopy, photograph, mag-
netic or other record, without the prior agreement and written
permission of the publisher.

Library of Congress Card Number: 92-83714
ISBN: 0-7821-1213-7

Manufactured in the United States of America
10 9 8 7 6 5 4 3 2 1

To LaVandra Russell

Acknowledgments

I'd like to thank Sunny Pinneau for thinking of me for this project, Dianne King for getting it going, and David Peal for his guidance during the early (and short) phases. I would also like to thank Guy Hart-Davis for his eagle eye and terrific sense of humor. Special thanks go to David Risher and his development team at Microsoft for creating Access and helping me understand its potential and capabilities.

Table of Contents

xiv

Appendix

Illustrations

Index

Introduction

This book covers the major features of Microsoft Access, the Windows product for designing and using databases. This book was written as a reference book for you to use as you work with Access, so we have kept the entries short and provided step-by-step instructions that will help you accomplish your task. The book does not include references to the Access Basic Language, which in itself could consume an entire volume.

This book can be used by those familiar with other database programs, as well as those new to databases. We do assume that you are familiar with the Windows environment. For example, we assume you know how to size and move windows.

ABOUT ACCESS

Access is Microsoft's first database product. It includes a graphical design environment for creating and modifying tables, forms, reports, queries, and macros. Access' graphical environment also lets you drag and drop objects from one area to another, join two or more tables by drawing a line between the common fields, and move and resize data on a form or report. Forms and reports can include graphics, such as a company logo. You can include OLE objects in records, so that a field in a record can actually contain sound, animation, a word-processing document, a spreadsheet, or a graphic image.

Access allows you to work with existing data—you can seamlessly import and export dBASE, FoxPro, ASCII text, Paradox, Btrieve, spreadsheet, and SQL Server data. You can even combine data from a variety of sources and file formats in the same Access database.

Access offers powerful Wizard tools that automate and simplify the creation of forms and reports—everything from a simple columnar report to mailing labels. Tool bars let you switch quickly between designing a form, report, or table, and viewing the results.

You can develop macros to perform repetitive tasks, or assign actions to buttons that you place on forms.

Access also offers some high-end features, such as referential integrity, self-joins (the ability to look up data in one field in the key field of the same table), and complex expressions and validation routines.

HOW TO USE THIS BOOK

This book has three parts:

Part I describes fundamental terms of databases, and provides a framework for the rest of the book.

Part II covers installing Access and Open Database Connectivity (OBDBC), starting and exiting Access, and using the mouse and the keyboard.

Part III contains reference material, arranged alphabetically. Numerous cross-references have been included to make your work easier.

The **Appendix** illustrates Access screens and buttons referred to throughout the text.

STYLISTIC AND TYPOGRAPHICAL CONVENTIONS

For clarity, we've used the following conventions in this book.

We show a series of menu options as a series of choices separated by ➤—for example: *Select File ➤ Open Database*. This means you should select File from the main menu (the list of options across the top of the screen), then select the Open Database option from the pulldown menu that appears. When appropriate, we've indicated which button on the tool bar accomplishes the same task.

We've used **boldface** to emphasize text that you may want to type in (for example, "enter the values directly: **Cash;Check;Charge**") and *italic* for text you see on the screen (for example, "press Tab or click on the box to the right of *Control Source*."). *Italic* also denotes cross references and important items.

Part I

Database Concepts

If you are new to databases, the next few pages are for you. They cover the basics you need to know to make the best use of Microsoft Access.

DATABASE MANAGEMENT SYSTEMS

Microsoft Access is a *database management system*, or DBMS. A DBMS allows you to collect and keep track of data about a particular subject, such as employees in a company or items in an inventory. In Access you store, retrieve, and manipulate data using the following *objects*, among others.

Object	Purpose
Table	To store data in a specific structure
Query	To locate stored data that meets certain criteria (for example, all employees in the state of Washington)
Form	To enter, display, modify, or delete data
Report	To display data on screen or paper

In Access, a *database* is a collection of objects that you create to keep track of information about a subject. You'd create an Employee database to store data about employees in your company in tables, update that information using forms, then do queries and print reports.

See Also   *Tables; Databases; Forms; Reports; Queries* in Part III

RECORDS AND FIELDS

Tables are divided into *records*, with one record for each unique person or thing. In an Employee table, you'd want to maintain data for

Jane Smith in one record and data for Paul Jones in another. Data in records is arranged in *fields*. In the Employee table, each field contains a particular bit of information about an employee, such as first name, last name, address, and employee number. You can think of fields as adjectives describing the person or thing.

All records have the same field structure, as shown in Figure I.1. The records for Jane Smith and Paul Jones, as well as for all other employees, contain a First Name field, a Last Name field, an Address field, and so on. Field *values* usually differ for each record. Jane Smith and Paul Jones have different values in the Employee Number field, but if they're married they'll have the same value in the Address field.

In Access you must define how data is stored in fields. For example, you would probably want to store a last name as text. Text is a *data type*. (In Access the Text data type lets you store both letters and numbers.) Since you might want to perform calculations on an employee's monthly salary, you'll want to store monthly salary

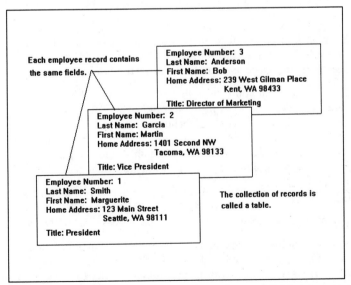

Figure I.1: All records in a database have the same field structure.

data in a data type that restricts a field to monetary amounts, so you would use the Currency data type for the Monthly Salary field. Access gives you many choices in defining the data type for a field. You can even define a field's data type as OLE Object, so you can store sounds, graphics, and entire Windows documents. (OLE [Object Linking and Embedding] allows you to place data from one application, such as a paint or drawing program, into another application, such as Access.)

See Also   *Records; Fields; Data Types* in Part III

FLAT-FILES VS. RELATIONAL TABLES

A *flat file* contains all information in a single table-like structure. Because a flat file is comprehensive, it's easy to use—but it also wastes disk space for the same reason.

Suppose that you need to keep information about an employee's dependents. *Every* record must contain enough fields to maintain the information for the employee with the most dependents.

Suppose also that you believe that an employee will have at most four dependents. In a flat file, you could create fields Dependent1, Dependent2, Dependent3, Dependent4. But you'd be wasting space in records for those employees who had no dependents, or just one or two. Then, when you hired an employee with five dependents, you couldn't enter data for the fifth dependent.

Some DBMSs allow you to separate data into multiple tables, then relate the tables to each other. Such DBMSs are called *relational* database management systems, or RDBMSs. Access is an RDBMS.

To track employees' dependents with Access, you might create two tables: an Employee table with information about employees only, and a Dependent table with information about dependents. To relate the tables, you would create in each table a field containing the same data.

For example, after defining an Employee Number field in the Employee table, you could create the same field in the Dependent table. This would tell Access to relate employees to their dependents using the Employee Number field. When you looked for Jane Smith, whose employee number is 5, you could identify her dependents by searching the Dependents table for records whose Employee Number field *also* contained a 5. Figure I.2 shows the relationship between two tables.

The employee number is used in both tables, but this duplication (or *redundancy*) usually wastes significantly less space than using a flat file. In a relational database, the Dependent table contains only information about dependents that exist. If Paul Jones has no dependents, there are no records in the Dependent table containing his employee number, so no space is lost.

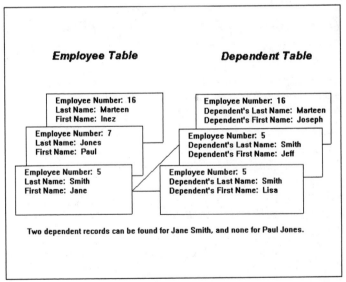

Figure I.2: The relationship between the Employee Table and the Dependent Table

FURTHER ADVANTAGES
OF A RELATIONAL SYSTEM

Suppose you need a list of all dependents ordered by their name and showing their home address. If you assume that each dependent has the same address as an employee, you can create a report using the first and last name from the Dependent table and address information from the Employee table. Rather than saving the home address information several times—once for each dependent, in the Dependent table—you save it once, in the Employee table.

Relating data simplifies the process of modifying, or updating, data. If an employee with three dependents moves to a different address, you only have to change the address in the Employee table—not the address for each dependent. The less you have to enter and update information, the fewer mistakes you're likely to make.

TYPES OF RELATIONSHIPS

Once you've created tables, Access allows you to define the relationship between them as *one-to-one* or *one-to-many*.

Suppose in addition to the Employee and Dependent tables you have a Job table that contains a list of each job code, the description of that code, and the minimum and maximum salary for the position.

You can relate the Employee table to the Job table using a one-to-one relationship, because one record in the Employee table can have only one job. While an employee may actually do more than one task, he or she is assigned a single job code, which can be found in the Jobs table.

Suppose, as in most large organizations, more than one employee can perform a similar task, such as a secretary, manager, or data-entry operator. In this case, it is possible to find more than one Employee record related to the same record in the Job table. That is, more than one Employee record contains the same job code. Now look at the relationship between the two tables from the perspective of the Job table. One record in the Job table can be related to one or more records in the Employee table. When you look at the relationship from the perspective of the Job table, you have a one-to-many relationship.

Thus, the type of relationship you have depends on the table that you look at first. In the case of the one-to-one relationship, you looked at the Employee table and examined how many records could be related to a single employee record, and found that only one job record could be so related. In the case of the one-to-many relationship, you looked at the Job table and examined how many Employee records could be related to a record in the Job table. The table that you examine first is called the *primary* table.

A third relationship is possible: a *many-to-many* relationship. For example, if a married couple work for a company and have two dependents, you will relate each spouse to both children. Thus one Employee record (the husband's record, for example), can be related to more than one record in the Dependent table. Likewise, a child can be related to more than one Employee (in this case, the child is related to the husband's Employee record *and* the wife's Employee record). A many-to-many relationship is shown in Figure I.3.

See Also   *Joining Tables; One-to-One Relationship; One-to-Many Relationship* in Part III

INDEXES AND KEY FIELDS

Access needs to know how your information is organized when it searches for values (as in a query) or when it sorts records. For example, you can find the employee record for *Grimaldi* by asking Access to search the entire table for "Grimaldi" (or even "Grim"). Access searches through every field of every record to find the right employee record.

You can reduce the time it takes Access to find a value by designating a field as an *index* or *key*. Say you define the Last Name field in your Employee table as an index. When you search for an employee's last name, Access uses the index to locate the record.

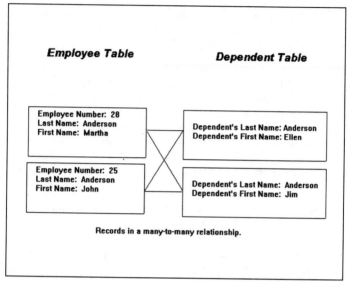

Figure I.3: A many-to-many relationship between Employee records and Dependent records

Using an index is much faster than looking through the entire table. When you add, change, or delete data in Access, indexes are updated automatically.

Like an index, a key speeds up searches in Access. Unlike an index, a key must contain a unique value for each record in the table. In the Employee table, no two employees can have the same employee number, so the employee number can serve as the key field for the table. You can use a key to automatically set one-to-many relationships between tables, since Access looks for key fields first to see whether the data types match.

Part II

Using Access

INSTALLING ACCESS

Before you can use Access, you must install it on your computer. You need an IBM-compatible PC with a 386-SX or higher processor and the following:

- 10 MB of free space on your hard disk;

- Windows 3.0 or 3.1; and

- at least 2 MB of RAM (4 MB or more is better).

Installing Access is straightforward and takes about 20 minutes.

To Install Access

To load Microsoft Access onto your hard disk:

1.   Start Windows.

2.   Insert Disk 1 in either drive A or drive B.

3.   Select File ➤ Run from the Program Manager's main menu. Enter **a:setup** or **b:setup**, depending on which drive contains the installation diskette, and select OK.

- Alternatively, open the File Manager and launch the SETUP.EXE file by double-clicking on it.

4.   Follow the instructions on the screen. Access asks for your name and the company name, the directory in which you want to install Access, and which part of Access you want to install (see the list below). Answer each question, then click on the Continue button.

If you cancel the installation at any point before Access provides the Installation Complete message, you must begin again at step 1.

During installation, Access offers you three options:

Complete	Installs all programs, help, cue cards, database drivers, Microsoft Graph, and sample files.
Custom	Lets you choose which parts of Access you want to install, including which database drivers you want to use.
Minimum	Installs the smallest number of files possible. For example, the mimimum installation does not install Help, Cue Cards, or sample files.

To Install ODBC

ODBC, *Open Database Connectivity*, lets you connect to Microsoft's SQL Server. To add this function to your Access program:

1. Start Windows.

2. Insert the ODBC setup disk in either drive A or drive B.

3. Select File ➤ Run from the Program Manager's main menu. Enter **a:setup** or **b:setup**, depending on which drive contains the ODBC installation diskette, and select OK.

4. Follow the instructions on the screen. Access asks you to select the available drivers. If an earlier version of the driver you want to install is listed in the Installed Drivers box, select it and choose Remove. Highlight the driver you want to install from the Available Drivers list, then select the Install-> button. The driver name is displayed in the Installed Drivers list. Select Continue.

5. Access copies the ODBC files to your hard disk, then asks if you want to add a new data source. The Setup Window is shown in Figure II.1. Select SQL Server from the Installed Driver list, then select Add New Name.

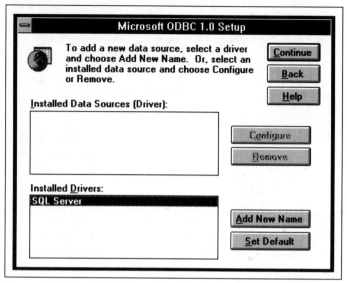

Figure II.1: The ODBC Setup Window

6. Enter the name of the server you want to be connected to in the Network Host text box. Change the Data Source Name and Description as appropriate, and select OK.

To Install Access on a Network

To install Access on a network server:

1. Connect to the network drive on which you want to install Access.

2. Start Windows if it is not already running.

3. Insert Disk 1 in either drive A or drive B.

4. Select File ➤ Run from the main menu.

5. Enter **a:setup /a** or **b:setup /a**, depending on which drive contains the installation diskette, and press Enter.

6. Follow the instructions on the screen. Access asks for your name, the directory in which you want to install Access, and which part of Access you want to install. Answer each question, then click on the Continue button.

• **NOTE**   You may need to be logged in to your network as supervisor to do the administrator install; this depends on the type of network and where you locate the Access files.

To Set Up a Workstation from a Network Server

To install Access on a workstation from the network server:

1. Connect to the network drive on which you installed Access.

2. Start Windows if it is not already running.

3. Select File ➤ Run from the main menu.

4. Enter **x:\access\setup /n**, where *x* is the network drive on which Access is installed. Press Enter.

5. Follow the instructions on the screen. When Access asks for the path for the SYSTEM.MDA file, use the path on the server if you want all users to be part of a workgroup. Otherwise, use a path name on the workstation.

• **NOTE**   A *workgroup* on a network is a group of users who share data as well as the same Access database.

STARTING ACCESS

We assume that you have already installed Microsoft Access on your hard disk. If not, see *Installing Access* above.

To Start Access

1. Start Windows.

2. Windows displays the Program Manager. Double-click on the Microsoft Access icon in the Microsoft Access group created during installation. See Figure II.2.

3. If Access displays the *Welcome to Microsoft Access* window, press Alt-C or click on the Close button. (To bypass this screen in future sessions, select the *Don't display this startup screen again* box.)

4. Select File ➤ Open Database and choose a database file in the Open Database dialog box. NWIND.MDB, for example, contains sample tables, queries, forms, reports, and macros. Select OK.

● **TIP** To open Access and automatically open a database, enter the database name after the program name. Click on the Access icon in the Program Manager, select File ➤ Properties, and add the program name in the Command Line box. For example, the command C:\ACCESS\ACCESS.EXE NWIND.MDB starts Access and opens the sample database NWIND.MDB.

● **TIP** You can also start Access by entering the database name with its path in the Run dialog box in the Program Manager, or by double-clicking on the database file in the File Manager.

Figure II.2: The Access icon

THE ACCESS DATABASE WINDOW

When you start Access and open a database, you will see the main window in Access, the Database window, shown in Figure A.1 in the Appendix.

In Access, a database is a set of objects that are related. You store the actual information (data) in Tables. With *queries*, you can find *dynasets*, subsets of this data, such as all employees in the state of Washington. You use *forms* to display and enter new records, or change or delete existing records. With *reports*, you can organize and display data on screen or on a printed page.

Along the left side of the opening screen is a set of six buttons, each representing a primary object in an Access database. When you select the button representing the type of object you want, Access displays a list of the available objects. For example, if you click on the Forms button, Access will display a list of forms in the database you opened. Figure A.1 shows the table button pressed; Access displays the list of tables already defined.

After selecting the type of object you want, you have three options. You can:

- select the New button to create a new object of that type;

- view the contents of the object, or the table the object is related to; or

- change the object itself.

USING THE MOUSE IN ACCESS

Access uses the standard mouse actions. For example, to move within a window that displays scroll bars, click on the up or down arrow keys in the scroll bar, move the scroll box, or press Page Up or Page Down to move to the next or previous screen.

Access displays some options in pull-down boxes or list boxes. To make a selection, press ↑ or ↓ until the option you want is highlighted, then press Enter, or click on the option.

Access does not use the secondary mouse button, which is usually the right mouse button.

USING THE KEYBOARD IN ACCESS

Access uses the following keyboard commands:

Action	Command
Add a new record	Ctrl-+
Copy selection to the Clipboard	Ctrl-C
Cut selection and place it on the Clipboard	Ctrl-X
Delete selection or next character to the left	Backspace
Delete selection or next character to the right	Delete
Delete the current record	Ctrl- -

Action	Command
Find the next occurrence of a string when Find or Replace dialog box is not displayed	Shift-F4
Help	F1
Insert a default value	Ctrl-Alt-spacebar
Insert a new line in a field, label, or zoom box	Ctrl-Enter
Insert current date	Ctrl-;
Insert current time	Ctrl-:
Insert value from the previous record	Ctrl-' or Ctrl-"
Move between the upper and lower parts of a window	F6
Move one *character* to the right	→
Move one *character* to the left	←
Move one *word* to the right	Ctrl- →
Move one *word* to the left	Ctrl- ←
Move to the beginning of a line	Home
Move to the end of a line	End
Move to the beginning of a field in a multi-line field	Ctrl-Home
Move to the end of a field in a multi-line field	Ctrl-End
Move to the next section of a form	F6
Move to the previous section of a form	Shift-F6

Action	Command
Move to the Record Number box (bottom of a window) in Datasheet view; go to page number in Print Preview mode	F5
Open a combo box	F4
Open a zoom box	Shift-F2
Paste the contents of the Clipboard	Ctrl-V
Recalculate fields	F9
Requery the tables in a query	Shift-F9
Save changes to current record	Shift-Enter
Select the current column	Ctrl-spacebar
Select the current record	Shift-spacebar
Switch between editing mode and navigation mode	F2
Undo changes	Esc
Undo typing	Ctrl-Z or Alt-Backspace

NAVIGATION IN A DATASHEET OR FORM

Use these commands to move about a datasheet or form:

Move one screen down	Page Down
Move one screen up	Page Up
Move one screen left (datasheet)	Ctrl-Page Up
Move one screen right	Ctrl-Page Down
Move to the first field of the current record	Home
Move to the last field of the current record	End

Move to the first field of the first record	Ctrl-Home
Move to the last field of the last record	Ctrl-End
Move to the next field of the current record	Tab or →
Move to the previous field of the current record	Shift-Tab or ←
Move to the next record (form)	Ctrl-Page Up
Move to the previous record (form)	Ctrl-Page Down
Move to the same field in the last record	Ctrl-↓
Move to the same field in the next record	↓
Move to the same field in the first record	Ctrl-↑
Move to the same field in the previous record	↑
Move from a subform to the next field of a main form	Ctrl-Tab
Move from a subform to the first field of a main form	Ctrl-Shift-Home

EXITING ACCESS

Double-click on the control menu box in the upper-left corner of the Microsoft Access window, or select File ➤ Exit from the main menu.

If any changed objects are in Design view and have not been saved, Access will ask if you want to save the changes or not. Answer Yes or No as appropriate. Access returns you to Windows.

Part III

Features and Functions

ACCESS WINDOW

When you start Access and open a database, Access displays the main Window. A status bar spans the bottom of the window, with seven small fields, shown in Figure A.1 of the Appendix. The status bar displays the following status indicators:

Indicator	Meaning
CAPS	Caps Lock is on
EXT	Extend mode is on (as when selecting one or more fields or records)
FLTR	A filter is applied to the displayed data; click on the Remove Filter button or select Records ➤ Show All Records to display all records
MOV	The move mode is activated (as when moving columns in a datasheet or query grid); press the Esc key to end move mode
NUM	Num Lock is on; press the Num Lock key to turn Num Lock off
OVR	Overtype mode is on (text you enter will replace existing text); press Ins to toggle between Overtype and Insert mode
SCRL	Scroll Lock is on; press the Scroll Lock key to turn Scroll Lock off

● **NOTE** EXT, FLTR, and MOV only appear when the operation in question is being performed. CAPS, NUM, and SCRL reflect the keyboard status. When the keyboard is in Insert mode, no indicator appears in the status line.

ACTION QUERIES

By default, Access queries are *select* queries, which means they display information but do not modify it. Unlike select queries, which can only display data, *action* queries let you change data in existing Access tables. There are four types of action queries:

Append queries	add a group of records from one table to another
Delete queries	delete a group of records
Make-table queries	create a new table based on another table
Update queries	change data in a table

To create an action query, open an existing query in Design view or create a new query, then click on the Action Query button. It looks like the Select Query button with an exclamation point (!) added (buttons are illustrated on the inside covers of this book).

To ensure that you modify the proper records, run a select query and examine the results before running an action query.

To Create an Append Query

To create an append query, create an action query to select data from existing tables and add new records at the end of another table (the receiving table).

1. Open a new query or an existing query. See *Queries* for more information. Figure A.5 in the Appendix shows a query window.

2. Select the tables that contain the data you want to append to the receiving table and select Add. Select Close when you have selected all needed tables.

3. Create or update the query's Query By Example (QBE) grid: Select all the fields you want appended to the receiving table, including the field that contains the data for the primary key in the receiving table. For more information about creating or modifying the QBE grid, see *Queries*. The QBE grid is shown in Figure A.5 in the Appendix.

4. Include in the QBE grid columns all fields used for limiting record selection, and include the criteria as appropriate.

5. Choose Query ➤ Select from the main menu and click on the Datasheet View button to verify your query. Click on the Design View button to return to the query definition.

6. Select Query ➤ Append. Select Current Database to add records to a table in the database you are using. Select the table to contain the records. Select Unique Values Only if you want to append only unique records. Select OK.

7. Enter the field in the receiving table for each field in the QBE grid in the Append To row.

8. Click on the Run button.

To Create a Delete Query

To define a new delete query:

1. Create a new query or open an existing query in Design view.

2. From the list box, select the tables that contain the data you want to delete, then select Close.

3. You must include an asterisk field from each table in the QBE grid to delete records in the table.

4. Enter criteria, if any, in the QBE grid.

5. Select Query ➤ Select from the main menu and click on the Datasheet View button to verify your query. Click on the Design View button to return to the query definition.

6. Select Query ➤ Delete.

7. The QBE grid changes the Delete row: the Delete row is added and the Sort and Show rows go away. It now shows From in all columns containing table names (and asterisks), and Where in all columns containing criteria.

8. Click on the Run button.

To Create a Make-Table Query

Create a new table following the steps in *To Create an Append Query* with one difference: In step 6 select Query ➤ Make Table and enter the name of the new table.

To Create an Update Query

To define a new update query:

1. Create a new query or open an existing query in Design view.

2. Select the table that contains the data you want to change, then select Close.

3. The columns in the QBE grid must contain the fields that will be updated and any fields used for criteria.

4. Enter criteria, if any, in the QBE grid.

5. Choose Query ➤ Select from the main menu and click on the Datasheet View button to verify your query. Click on the Design View button to return to the query definition.

6. Select Query ➤ Update.

7. In the Update To row in the QBE grid, enter the new value for each field to be changed.

8. Click on the Run button.

See Also *Criteria; Parameter Queries; Queries; Select Queries*

ATTACH A DATABASE FILE

If you attach a database from dBASE or Paradox, or a table from Btrieve, you instruct Access to read and write data to the original database. No copy is made, and the original database is not converted to Access's own format.

When you import data from another format (Btrieve, dBASE, or Paradox, for example), you copy it to Access and save it in Access's own format. You work with a *copy* of the file in Access, *not* the original file.

See Also *Import a Database File*

BORDERS

Borders provide a visual guide to objects in the screen. For example, you might use dark, wide borders to highlight fields.

To Change the Border of a Control

To change the thickness and style of a control's border on a form or report:

1. Select the control(s) you want to change.

- To select a single control, click on it.
- To select more than one control, press and hold down Shift while you select the controls.
- If the controls are all in a rectangular area, click on the arrow in the toolbox and drag a rectangle around the area.

2. Select the Palette button from the tool bar, or select View ➤ Palette from the main menu. The Palette window appears (see Figure III.1).

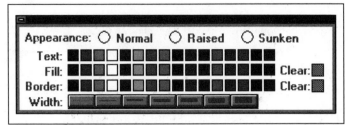

Figure III.1: The Palette window

3. Click on a color in the Border row.

4. Click in the Clear box at the end of the Border row if you want the border to be transparent.

5. Select the border size from the buttons in the Width line.

6. Click on the Palette button or select View ➤ Palette again.

See Also   *Controls*

BTRIEVE

Btrieve keeps information about its databases in what it calls an Xtrieve dictionary file (the filename is FILE.DDF). You need to know the location of the Xtrieve dictionary file in order to export Btrieve data.

To Save a Table in Btrieve Format

To save an Access table in Btrieve format:

1. Open the database containing the table you want to export.

2. Switch to the database window by pressing F11.

3. Select File ➤ Export. In the Export dialog box, choose Btrieve in the Data Destination box. Select OK.

4. In the Select Microsoft Access Object dialog box, select the table you want to export, then click on OK.

5. In the Export to File dialog box, find the Xtrieve dictionary file (FILE.DDF) and select OK.

6. Enter the name of the new Btrieve table, then select OK.

● **NOTE** You cannot create the Btrieve dictionary file in Access.

To Use a Btrieve File

To attach or import a file from a Btrieve table, you must provide the Xtrieve dictionary file before you can specify the Btrieve table.

When you import a file, you convert the data to Access' format. When you attach a file, you use the original file in its original format, not a copy of the file.

To use a Btrieve file:

1. Be sure a Microsoft Access database is open.

2. Select File ➤ Attach Table from the main menu to attach a Btrieve table. Select File ➤ Import to import a Btrieve table.

3. Select Btrieve as the Data Source.

4. Specify the Xtrieve dictionary file (FILE.DDF).

5. In the Tables box, select the table you want, then select Import or Attach.

6. If the Btrieve table was saved with a password, Access will prompt you for the password.

7. Microsoft Access creates the table automatically if you are importing the Btrieve table, or adds the table to the list of tables if you are attaching the Btrieve table. Repeat steps 5 and 6 until you have selected all needed tables.

8. Set a primary key if necessary.

Access converts some Btrieve data types to types it can use. Access performs the following conversions:

Btrieve data type	Access data type (FieldSize Property)
Bfloat	Number (Double)
Date	Date/Time
Float	Number (Double)
Integer (1 byte)	Number (Byte)
Integer (2 byte)	Number (Integer)
Integer (4 byte)	Number (Long integer)
Logical	Yes/No
Lstring	Text
Lvar	OLE Object
Money	Currency
Note	Memo
String	Text
Time	Date/Time
Zstring	Text

See Also *Attach a Database File; Export a Table; Import a Database File*

BUTTONS

Buttons are a common feature of a graphical user interface (GUI). When you click on a button, Access performs a predefined task, such as displaying the next record.

To Create a Button on a Form

To create a new button on a form:

1. Open the form in Design view. See *Design View* for more information. An empty form in Design view is shown in Figure A.7 in the Appendix.

2. In the toolbox, select the button tool from the tool bar (illustrated on the inside covers), then point and drag over the location on the form where you want a button.

3. To assign a macro to the button, click on the button to select it, then click on the Properties button in the tool bar or select View ➤ Properties from the main menu. Use Tab to move to the right of *On Push* (or click directly in the cell) and enter the name of the macro.

   - If the macro is part of a macro group, enter the group name, a period, and the macro name in the On Push property.

   - Alternatively, click at the end of the cell and select the macro you want to assign to the button from the list of available macros that Access displays.

You can also create a button and assign a macro to it directly by using Access' drag-and-drop feature:

1. Open the form in Design View. See *Design View* for more information.

2. Open the Database window by pressing F11.

3. In the Database window, click on the Macro button. Select the macro you want to assign to the button.

4. Drag the macro name to the form and release the mouse button. Access creates the button and assigns the macro name to the On Push property.

5. To change the text on the button's face, click on the Properties button in the tool bar or select View ➤ Properties from the main menu. Change the button's Caption property.

To Place a Picture on a Button

To replace the face of a button with a bitmap:

1. Open the form in Design view. See *Design View* for more information.

2. Select the button on which you want to place the bitmap. If no picture has been assigned to the button, the Picture property displays *(none)*.

3. In the Properties window, enter the complete file name, including drive, directory, and file name, of the bitmap in the Picture property. Bitmap files have the file extension .BMP.

4. When set, the property value changes to *(bitmap)*, and the face of the button is replaced by the bitmap image.

To Delete a Bitmap from a Button's Face

To delete a bitmapped image:

1. Open the form in Design view. See *Design View* for more information.

2. Select the button whose bitmap you want to delete.

3. In the Properties window select the entire text in the Picture property. The Picture property should display *(bitmap)*.

4. Press Del. Press Tab or click outside the property cell.

5. Access will ask if you want to delete the graphic from the button. Select OK.

See Also *Forms; Macros*

CALCULATIONS

A calculated control contains the result of an arithmetic operation (such as addition or multiplication) using existing fields (such as Payment Amount), functions (such as Average), and constants (such as 1.23). The calculation performed is stored in an expression that is assigned to the Control Source property of a control on a form or report. Calculated fields are for display only—they cannot be edited in Form view.

To Add a Calculated Control to a Form or Report

To add a control that performs calculations to a form or report:

1. Open the form or report in Design view. See *Design View* for more information.

2. Add a control, such as a text box, to the form or report. See *Controls* for more information.

3. Be sure the control is selected: The mouse pointer appears as a vertical bar when it is over the selected control.

   - If the object is not a check box, option button, or option group, enter the expression in the control. (You can also enter the expression directly in the Control Source property.)

   - If the object is a check box, option button, or option group, enter the expression directly in the Control Source Property.

4. To view or change the Properties box, select View ➤ Properties from the main menu or click on the Properties button in the tool bar. You must use this technique if the control is a check box, option button, or option group.

See Also   *Controls; Expressions*

CHECK BOXES

A check box control indicates whether a value is on or off, true or false, selected or not selected. An *X* appears in the box when the value is on, true, or selected; the box is empty when the value of the field it represents is off, false, or not selected.

To Add a Check Box to a Form

To add a check box to represent the value of a field:

1. Open the form in Design view. See *Design View* for more information.

2. Choose the Checkbox button from the toolbox. The toolbox is illustrated on the inside front cover.

3. Select the field name from the Field List. (If the Field List is not displayed, select View ➤ Field List.) The field type of the selected field should be Yes/No or Number.

4. Drag the field to the form. Access includes a default label to the right of the check box.

To Add an Unbound Check Box to a Form or Report

You can create an *unbound* check box (one that is not tied to a field). Such check boxes can represent the value of an expression—for example, whether the total amount of an order is over a specified limit and therefore must be verified.

To add an unbound check box:

1. Open the form in Design view. See *Design View* for more information.

2. Choose the Checkbox button from the toolbox. The toolbox is illustrated on the inside front cover.

3. Click on the area to contain the control.

4. Enter the expression in the Control Source property of the Property window. If the Property window is not visible, click on the Properties button or select View ➤ Properties from the main menu.

● **TIP** If the field represented by a check box has a Numeric data type, the value −1 is the same as true (or yes), and 0 is the same as false (or no).

See Also *Controls; Option Groups; Forms*

COLORS

You can set the color of objects, such as text on a report or input fields on a form, using the color palette. You can use color to draw attention to special information or sections of a report or form.

To Set the Color(s) of an Object

To set the text, fill, and border color(s) of an object:

1. Select the object(s) you want to change. Access calls these objects controls. To select multiple controls, select the first control, then hold down Shift while you select the remaining controls.

2. Select the Palette button from the tool bar.

3. Set the text, fill, and border colors. If you want, you can select the border width.

4. Select special effects such as Sunken or Raised.

5. Select the Palette button or double-click on the Control menu box to close the palette window.

The following properties can be used in Design view to set color:

Property	Where color is applied
BackColor	For sections in forms and reports, and tools (such as graphs) and controls, sets the interior color (for example, the interior of a sunken text box); for large areas (such as a screen), BackColor refers to the background color
BackStyle	Sets the transparency of a control or tool; settings are *normal* to use the same color as the BackColor property, and *clear* to use the background color of the form or report
BorderColor	Sets the color of a control's border (note: the Special Effect property must be Normal to use BorderColor; if the Border Style and BackStyle properties are modifiable, they must be Normal also)

See Also   *Controls; Properties*

COLUMNS

Datasheets and query grids are arranged in columns. Access lets you adjust all columns in the same way.

To Change the Width of a Column

To make a column wider or narrower:

1.   Click on the border separating the column from the column to its right. The pointer changes to a double-headed arrow with a vertical line down the middle.

2.   Drag the double-headed arrow to the location of the column border and release the mouse button.

To Hide or Display a Column

To hide a column:

1. Select the column header of the column or columns you want to hide.

2. Select Layout ➤ Hide Columns.

To unhide a column:

1. Select Layout ➤ Show Columns.

2. Select the columns you want to unhide (display). Visible columns are displayed with a check in the list.

3. Select Show.

4. Select Close.

To Freeze or Unfreeze Columns

When you move to the left or right of a datasheet, columns will normally disappear to make room to display new columns. Keeping a column visible when you scroll vertically can help you keep track of which record you're viewing. Here's how to do this:

1. Select the column or columns you want to keep on the left side of the display by clicking on the column's heading.

2. Select Layout ➤ Freeze Columns.

To return to normal view (with no columns frozen), select Layout ➤ Unfreeze All Columns.

To Rearrange Columns

To change the order of columns using the mouse:

1. Move the mouse pointer to the top of the columns you want to move so that it changes to a solid, down-pointing arrow.

2. Click on the column headings. The columns appear in reverse video.

3. Click and drag the column heading to the column heading of the new location. For example, to move the column one column to the left, drag the selected column's heading to the heading of the column one column to the left.

4. The pointer displays a small box attached to an arrow. When the small box is positioned inside the column heading of the new location, release the mouse button. The existing columns are shifted to the right.

To change the order of columns using the keyboard:

1. Click on the headings of the columns you want to move.

2. Press Ctrl-F8. *MOV* appears in the status bar at the bottom of the datasheet.

3. Press the right arrow to move the column to the right. Press the left arrow to move the column to the left.

4. Press Esc to leave move mode.

To Save Layout Changes

To save changes to the column layout from within a Table window, select File ➤ Save Layout. To save the changes from within a Form window, select File ➤ Save Form.

See Also   *Datasheets; Grids*

COMBO BOXES

A combo box allows you to enter a field value into a text box or select a value from a list that drops down from the box itself. Combo boxes are useful data entry shortcuts.

Figure III.2 illustrates a combo box.

To Create a Combo Box with Predefined Values

To define a combo box and define the valid values:

1. Open the form in Design view. See *Design View* for more information.

2. Select the combo box tool from the toolbox (illustrated on the inside front cover).

3. To create a combo box bound to a field, select the field from the Field window and drag the field name to the form. This will set the Control Source property of the option group to the field name. Go to step 5.

4. To create a combo box in an unbound option group, click on the form where you want the combo box to appear. You must manually set the expression within the Control Source property for the option group. See *Properties* for information on specifying properties.

5. Select the combo box.

6. Open the Properties window by clicking on the Properties button in the tool bar or selecting View ➤ Properties from the main menu.

7. Select the Row Source Type property and set it to Value List.

Figure III.2: A combo box in Form view

8. To display a single-column drop-down list, select the Row
Source property and enter the values directly, separated
by a semicolon. For example: **Cash;Check;Charge**

- To display a multicolumn drop-down list, enter the
  number of columns in the Column Count property.
  Select the Row Source property and enter the values
  directly, each separated by a semicolon. The number of
  values must be divisible by the number of columns. For
  example, in a two-column table that contains a payment method and payment code, enter:
  Cash;100;Check;200;Charge;300

- In a multicolumn drop-down list, the Bound Column
  property refers to the column that contains the value to
  be displayed in the combo box when a selection is
  made. Thus, in the payment example, set the Bound
  Column property to 1 to display the text of the payment method; set the Bound Column property to 2 to
  display the payment code.

CREATING COMBO BOXES THAT
LOOK UP VALUES IN OTHER QUERIES OR TABLES

You can have Access look up the values in a table or query when
you click on the Combo Box. The pull-down list displays the first
field in the table or query you use. If you want to display a field
other than the first field, you must create a custom query.

To Create a Combo Box with Lookup Values

To define a combo box that displays values from a table or query:

1. Open the form in Design view. See *Design View* for more
information.

2. Select the combo box tool from the tool box (illustrated on
the inside front cover).

3. To create a combo box bound to a field, select the field
from the Field window and drag the field name to the
form. This sets the Control Source property of the option
group to the field name.

4.   To create a combo box in an unbound option group, click on the form where you want the combo box to appear. You must manually set the expression within the Control Source property for the option group.

5.   Select the combo box.

6.   Open the Properties window by clicking on the Properties button in the tool bar or selecting View ➤ Properties from the main menu.

7.   Select the Row Source Type property and set it to Table/Query. Select the Row Source property and select the table or query that contains the values to be displayed in the pull-down list. The pull-down list will display the first field from the table or query.

● **TIP**   To display a multicolumn drop-down list, set the Column Count property to the number of columns you want to display. The Bound Column property refers to which column (of those displayed in the pull down list) contains the value to be displayed in the combo box when a selection is made.

● **TIP**   You can use *structured query language* (SQL) statements instead of a query as the lookup source. SQL statements execute somewhat faster than queries.

To Use SQL Statements in Combo Boxes

To use SQL statements as the expression for combo boxes:

1.   Create a query. In Design view, select View ➤ SQL from the main menu. Figure III.3 shows the SQL text window.

2.   Select the SQL statement displayed in the SQL text window and copy it to the Windows Clipboard. When the SQL window is active, you cannot select the Edit menu: instead, use Ctrl-C to copy to the Clipboard.

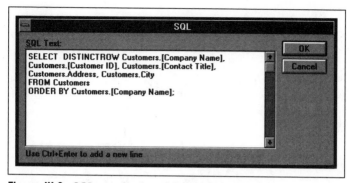

Figure III.3: SQL text displayed in an SQL window

3. Open the form containing the combo box in Design view. See *Design View* for more information. Select the Row Source property and press Ctrl-V to paste the contents of the Clipboard into the property value. This tells Access what information is requested.

4. Set the Row Source Type property to Table/Query. This tells Access to display values from a table or query rather than from a predefined list.

See Also *SQL Databases; SQL Statements*

To Create Combo Boxes That Display a List of Field Names

To create a combo box that displays a list of a table's or query's field names:

1. Follow steps 1 through 6 in *To Create a Combo Box with Look Up Values* above.

2. Select the Row Source Type property and set it to Field List.

3. Set the Row Source property to the query or table containing the field names.

● **TIP** To hide a column, set the Column Widths property. Column Widths contains a number for each column's widths, separated by a semicolon. Use a width of 0 to hide a column.

● **TIP** To restrict the combo box to accept only displayed values (no new values can be entered during data entry), set the Limit To List property to Yes.

COMPACTING A DATABASE

Compacting a database defragments it. Fragmenting can occur when a database is updated. When you compact a database, you can either replace the current version or save the compacted database to a new file.

To Compact a Database

To defragment a database:

1. Close the database if it is open. The database must be closed by *all* users in a multiuser environment.

2. Close the Database window. Access' screen displays two menus: File and Help. The rest of the window is empty.

3. Go to the File Manager (or a third-party utility) and make a copy of the database to be compacted in another directory in case compacting fails.

4. Return to Access and select File ➤ Compact Database.

5. Select the file name of the database you want to compact. Database files have the extension .MDB. Access suggests a new file name.

6. If you enter the file name of the existing file, Access will warn you that the file already exists and ask you if you wish to replace the existing file. Select Yes to overwrite the file, or No to enter a different file name.

7. Access displays a progress indicator in the status bar at the bottom of the window. The program displays a dialog box indicating success or failure upon completion of the task.

CONTROLS

Controls are objects added to a form or report: a graph, picture (such as a logo), field from a table, or text used as a label for a field or a heading of a report. Although all these objects are called controls, only button controls actually control any action. Controls are used to display data from a record, provide a heading on a report, or display a bitmap of a logo on a form.

Controls are the building blocks of forms and reports. For example, you must have one control for each field in a table you want to display on a form or report.

Bound and Unbound Controls

A *bound* control is one that is linked to a field in a table—it displays data from a table. An *unbound* control is one that is not linked to a field. On a form, for example, data entered by a user as a parameter to a query is an example of an unbound control. A label on a form is another example of an unbound control.

To Add, Move, or Delete Controls on a Form or Report

Everything on a form or report is a control. Fields (bound or unbound to a table or query), graphs, text, and control buttons are all controls. Figure A.8 in Appendix shows a form with several controls for the Customers table, a sample table provided with Access.

The following steps show you how to manipulate controls on an Access form or report.

1. Open a form or report in Design view. See *Design View* for instructions.

2. Select the type of control you want to add from the tool-box (illustrated on the inside front cover). For example, select a text box, command button, or label.

3. If you selected a text box tool or bound object frame tool in step 2, you can click on a field from the Table window and drag the field name to the form. (If the window is not open, click on the Field List button in the tool bar, or select View ➤ Fields from the main menu.)

4. Move the mouse to the form. Click on the upper-left corner of the control, and drag button to the bottom-right corner. Release the mouse.

5. Access may ask you further questions about your control, depending on which type of control you selected. For example, if you insert an object (using the unbound object frame button in the toolbox), Access will ask you to identify the object type and the file name.

● **TIP**   If you want to add a field with an OLE data type (a field that can store documents, sounds, and other objects), select the bound object frame tool in step 2. In Design view, the object appears as an empty box—no image is displayed. The image *is* retrieved from the individual record and displayed in the control when you are in Form or Report view. Furthermore, in Form or Report view, double-clicking on the object launches the OLE server application and lets you modify the object.

To Add a Group of Controls

With the Duplicate command, you can add a group of controls that are the same size and shape and are evenly spaced on a form or report. This command is useful for evenly spacing buttons and check boxes.

1. Open the form or report in Design view. See *Design View* for more information.

2. Select a control by clicking on it in the toolbox.

3. Open the Properties window by clicking on the Properties button in the tool bar or selecting View ➤ Properties from the main menu.

4. Set a control's properties by entering the desired value in the cell to the right of the property's name, as appropriate.

5. Select Edit ➤ Duplicate.

6. If the control is *not* in an option group, Access creates a copy of the control and places it on top of the original control. Move the *new* control to its new location and select Edit ➤ Duplicate. If the control *is* in an action group, Access displays the new control underneath the original control.

7. Access displays a third control aligned with the first two controls.

● **NOTE** Option groups are sets of buttons or check boxes that comprise a set of alternatives—only one control within a group can be selected.

To Add a Label to a Control

After you position the label, the mouse pointer turns into an I-beam. Type the text for the label. When you are done, click anywhere outside the label. Access automatically wraps text to fit the size of the control.

If you want the label to have more than one line of text, press Ctrl-Enter to begin a new line.

● **NOTE** A label is a box containing text that describes the contents of the adjacent control, such as Name or City.

To Move a Control

1. Click on the control. Handles like black dots surround the control and an icon of a dark open hand appears over the control.

2. Click anywhere inside the outline, drag button to move the control, and release the mouse when the control is in the desired location.

● **TIP** Hold down Shift to select the multiple controls.

To Resize a Control

To change the size of a control:

1. Click on the control.

2. When the black dots surround the control, move the pointer to a black dot. When the pointer changes to a two-headed arrow, click and drag the outline to a new size.

To Delete a Control

To remove a control from a form or report:

1. Click on the control to select it.

2. Press Del or select Edit ➤ Delete from the main menu.

To Change the Appearance and Behavior of a Control

You can modify controls in several ways. For example, you can change the color and 3-D effect of a control by selecting the Palette button in the tool bar and clicking on the options you want. (See *Colors* for more information). Likewise, you can change the text within a label control by changing its Caption property.

For more information about setting properties of controls, see *Properties, To Set a Property*.

To Combine Text and a Function in a Control

You can combine text and the result of a function in a single control
to give a function value the appearance of a label. For example, instead of displaying only the current date in the page header section,
you can combine text and the results of the Now() function, or you
can change the field in the page header section to read *Report Date
and Time:* followed by the date and time. To do so, you work with
the control's Control Source property.

1. Be sure the report or form is in Design view. See *Design
    View* for more information. If you are in Report Preview
    mode, select Cancel.

2. Click on the control you want to change, or add a new text
    box control and click on it.

3. Open the properties window by clicking on the View
    Properties button in the tool bar (the third button from the
    left in the tool bar), or select View ➤ Properties from the
    main menu.

4. The second box in the Text Box window provides space for
    you to enter the new value of the Control Source property.
    Control Source refers to the location or contents of the text
    box. For example, the Control Source of a report date con-
    trol is set at =Now() by the ReportWizard.

5. Press Tab or click on the box to the right of *Control Source*.
    Press Shift-F2 to open the Zoom window, which provides
    a larger window in which to enter the Control Source
    value. The text is highlighted in reverse video.

6. Enter the expression. For example, enter an = sign, your
    text (surrounded in quotes), the & symbol, and a function
    for the date as: **="Report Date: " & Now()**. Access reads
    the expression as follows:

    The **equal sign** means that the contents of the control will
    be replaced by what follows.

    "Report Date: " is text that will appear in the field when it
    is printed or displayed.

    The **&** tells Access to concatenate "Report Date: " with the
    current date and time, which is supplied by Now().

7. Select OK. The Control Source property cell is replaced by the contents of the Zoom window.

To Modify a Control's Label

By default, Access includes a bound control's label when you add the control to a form or report. Access considers the control and its label as a group: when you click on the control, you select both the field *and* its label.

To modify a control's label, click on the label to select it. You can now modify the label, or click on the control itself to work with it.

To Align Controls on a Form to Each Other

To align controls along a common border:

1. Hold down Shift and select the controls to be aligned.

2. Select Layout ➤ Align from the main menu.

3. Select the edge of the controls to be aligned (left, right, top, or bottom).

To Align Controls on a Form to a Grid

To align controls to predefined grid lines:

1. Open the form in Design view. See *Design View* for more information.

2. If the grid is not displayed, select View ➤ Grid from the main menu.

3. If you are adding a new control, select Layout ➤ Snap to Grid from the main menu.

4. To align existing objects to the grids, select the control(s), then select Layout ➤ Size to Grid from the main menu. This may cause the controls to change their size slightly.

To Use a Control as a Model for Other Controls

If you add several controls of the same type to a form, you can set the characteristics (size, shape, and font, for example) of one of the controls and use this as the model for existing or new controls of the same type.

To apply the control's characteristics to new controls:

1. Select the control.

2. Select Layout ➤ Change Default from the main menu.

To apply the control's characteristics to existing controls of the same type:

1. Select the control.

2. Select Layout ➤ Change Default from the main menu.

3. Select the control you want to change, then select Layout ➤ Apply Default from the main menu.

• To apply the default to more than one existing control, press and hold Shift while you select the controls.

See Also   *Option Groups; Forms; Reports; Colors; Borders; Properties; Labels*

CONTROL MESSAGES ON STATUS BAR

When adding a control to a form, set the control's Status Bar Text property to the text you want displayed when the control is edited during data entry. The property defaults to the field's name.

See Also   *Properties*

COPY A DATABASE OBJECT TO ANOTHER DATABASE

To save design time, you can copy a table, query, form, etc., to another database.

To Copy an Object to Another Database

To copy one Access database object (table, query, etc.) to another Access database:

1. Open the Database window by pressing F11.

2. Select File ➤ Export from the main menu.

3. In the Data Destination dialog box, select Microsoft Access, then select OK.

4. In the Object Type box, select the table or database object you want to export. If you are exporting a table, select whether you want to export only the structure or the structure and data together. In the Objects box, select the object you want to export.

5. When Access displays the Export to File dialog box, enter the name of the Access database that you want to contain the database object. This database must already exist.

6. Enter the name the object will have in the database and select OK.

See Also   *Compacting a Database*

COUNTING RECORDS

To display a count of the number of records in a table (or subset as defined by a query):

1. Open the query in Design view. See *Design View* for more information.

2. If the *Total:* row is not displayed in the QBE grid at the bottom of the window, select View ➤ Totals in the main menu.

3. In the *Total:* row, click in the box in the Field column and select Count.

4. Run the query by clicking on the Run button in the tool bar (the one with the exclamation point on it) or by selecting Query ➤ Run from the main menu.

See Also   *Grids*

CRITERIA

Criteria are used to select records in queries and filters. Criteria set the conditions that must be matched in order for a record to be included in a dynaset.

To Create Criteria

To add criteria to a query:

1. Open a query in Design view. See *Design View* for more information. Figure A.5 in the Appendix shows an empty query.

2. Click on the Set Filter button in the tool bar or select Records ➤ Edit Filter/Sort from the main menu. The filter window is shown in Figure A.10 in the Appendix.

3. If the field used for comparison has not been included in the grid at the bottom of the query window, drag it from the field list to a new column in the Field row.

4. Select the cell in the Criteria row underneath the field heading of the field used for comparing values. For example, to select parts with prices less than $1.00, select the cell in the Criteria row in the Price column.

5. Enter the criteria expression. For example, to find customers that live in California, enter **"CA"** (including the quotation marks) in the Criteria row of the State column.

6. If you want to enter one of several criteria a field must meet in order to include the record in the filter or query, enter the *"or"* condition in the cell beneath the first criteria expression. For example, to select all customers who are doctors or lawyers, enter **"doctor"** (including the quotation marks) in the Profession field's Criteria box, and enter **"lawyer"** in the cell immediately underneath *"doctor."* *"Lawyer"* appears in the *Or* row.

7. Fields used in criteria expressions are displayed in the dynaset. (A *dynaset* is a subset of fields and records that you can edit as though you were working with an entire table or group of related tables.) To use the field in such expressions but exclude it from the dynaset, click on the Show box so it is not selected (the check box is empty).

Access may display your criteria expression in a format slightly different from that used when the data was entered. For example, if you enter the expression <7/1/94 in the criteria for a field of data type Date/Time, Access translates it to <#7/1/94#, since dates in expressions must be surrounded by the # character. Similarly, text strings will be surrounded by quotes when values include embedded blanks, such as "New Jersey" or "Price Per Unit".

To add criteria to a filter, open a form in Datasheet view or Form view, see the Tip below, and follow steps 2–6 above.

See Also   *Expressions*

● **TIP**   To set criteria that meet the opposite of a value, use the Not operator. For example, to find customers that are not doctors, enter **Not "doctors"** in the Criteria row of the Professions field.

To Use Criteria in Totals Calculations

Your criteria can specify which records to include in calculations that compute totals.

To limit the groupings, enter the criteria fields in columns that use Group By in the Total row. If you enter **> 1000** in the Order field's Criteria cell, Access selects all records in which the order field's value is $1000 or more. Thus, all records in which an order was greater than $1000 or more are included in the dynaset.

To set the criteria on the *total* value of a field, enter the criteria field in columns that use an aggregate function (such as Sum) in the Total row. If you enter **>1000** in the Order field's Criteria cell, Access adds up the total value of all orders for a customer; if the total amount of the all orders for the customer in the table is over $1000, the customer records are included in the dynaset.

To set the criteria of the records that should be included in the total value for a field, set the Total row to Where and enter the criteria in the Criteria Row. If you enter **> 1000** in the Order field's Criteria cell in this case, Access sums up only those records in which an in-dividual order is over $1000, and includes the total for orders over $1000 in the dynaset.

To set the Totals value:

1. Open a query in Design view. See *Design View* for more information.

2. Click on the totals button on the tool bar (marked with a sigma, Σ) or select View ➤ Totals from the main menu. The tool bar is shown in the inside front cover.

3. Select the Total option you want (such as Sum).

● **NOTE**   *Wildcards* such as ? and * allow you to select records whose fields match a pattern. Wildcards can be used on fields that are of data type Text or Date/Time. For a complete list of wildcard characters, see *Expressions, The Like Operator*.

See Also   *Grids; Wildcards; Filters*

CROSSTABS

Crosstabs can be used with aggregate functions to display a field value (sum, count, average, etc.) in row and column format. Crosstabs are generally used to summarize data, not show each record. Given the proper data in a table, crosstabs can show the total number of parts sold by state by quarter, or average rainfall by state by month.

To Create a Crosstab

Before you create a crosstab, you must decide which field to use as the column heading, which field to use as the row heading, and which field to summarize (the value field).

1. Create a new query. See *Queries* for complete instructions.

2. Select the tables that contain the information to be used in the crosstab. Select Close when you have selected all tables.

3. If you are using multiple tables, join the common fields.

4. Select Query ➤ Crosstab from the main menu. The window changes to include crosstab options; a row is added to the QBE grid. The window, using sample data from a sample table, is shown in Figure A.14 in the Appendix.

5. To add the column heading for an existing field, drag the field from the proper table window to the Field row of the first column.

- The Total cell should display Select Group. (If it doesn't display Select Group, set it so that it does.)
- Set the Crosstab cell to Column Heading.

- If the table windows are not displayed, select View ➤ Table Names from the main menu.

- To group values in a column, see *Grouping Data in Columns* below.

- You can also use an expression as the column field. Enter the expression in the Field cell.

6. To add the row heading, drag the field from the table to the Field row of the next column. The Total cell should display Select Group (set it if it does not). Set the Crosstab cell to Row Heading. You can also use an expression as the row field. Enter the expression in the Field cell.

7. Select the field whose value you want to summarize from the table at the top of the query, and drag it to the next empty column. This is called the value field. Click on the Crosstab cell and select Value.

8. Click in the Total cell of the same column. Select the calculation you want. See *Calculation Types* later in this section.

9. To add a grand total column, you must add a calculated field to the QBE grid. In the Field cell of a new column, enter the new field name and the value field, separated by a colon. (For example, **Grand Total:Employee Earnings**.) In the Crosstab cell, select Row Heading; in the Total cell, enter the type of total you want.

10. Click on the Datasheet button or Run button in the tool bar to display the results of the crosstab.

● **TIP**   If a row heading contains <>, the value in the crosstab cell was derived from records that have no value in the row field.

To Save a Crosstab

To save a crosstab for future use:

1. If the crosstab query is in Datasheet view, select File ➤ Save Query. If the crosstab query is in Design view, select File ➤ Save.

2. If this is the first time you have saved the crosstab query, Access asks you to name the query. Enter the query name and select OK.

To Save a Crosstab Using a Different Name

To keep a copy of a modified crosstab separate from the original crosstab you edited, select File ➤ Save As (in Design view) or File ➤ Save Query As (in Datasheet view). Enter the new query name for the crosstab and select OK.

To Run a Crosstab from the Database Window

To execute a crosstab while the Database window is displayed:

1. Move to the Database window by pressing F11.

2. Click on the Query button. Access lists all queries, including crosstab queries, in the same list.

3. Highlight the crosstab query you want to run.

4. Double-click on the query name, or select the Open button.

5. Access displays the results of the crosstab query in a Datasheet.

Calculation Types

Access can perform a variety of calculations either automatically (by selecting a type in a crosstab) or by explicitly setting a calculation in a property box.

Calculation	What calculation does
Avg	Compute the average value
Count	Count the number of records a query selects.
Expression	Evaluate an expression for this field
First	Display the value in the first record (using the current sort order)

Calculation	What calculation does
Group By	The default; this performs no calculation
Last	Display the value in the last record (using the current sort order)
Max	Find the largest (maximum) value
Min	Find the smallest (minimum) value
StDev	Compute the standard deviation
Sum	Add all values
Var	Compute the variance of all values
Where	Specifies a limiting expression; fields that use the Where value are not displayed; where values are used to restrict records in a crosstab

To Set Column Order

By default, crosstabs display columns in ascending order (a–z). While this works well for most Date/Time and Text fields, it arranges data alphabetically rather than by month when monthly summaries are requested (April, August, February, etc.).

To fix the order of the columns based on their value:

1. With the query in Design view, select the columns whose order you want to control. See *Design View* for more information on opening a query in Design view.

2. Select the fixed column headings box. Figure III.4 shows the Query Properties dialog box and Fixed Column Headings box

3. Check the Fixed Column Headings box so that an X appears.

4. In the box at the bottom of the Query Properties dialog box enter the column names in the order in which you want them to appear, separated by semicolons. Alternatively, enter one column name per line by entering a

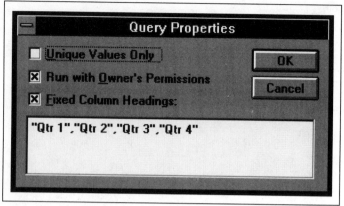

Figure III.4: The Querie Properties dialog box.

> column name, then pressing Ctrl-Enter to begin a new
> line. If a column name is more than one word, surround
> the name in quotation marks.

5. Select OK.

To Suppress Repeating Entries

To display a value only once in a crosstab:

1. Click on the Properties box in the tool bar or select View ➤
   Query Properties from the main menu.

2. Check the Unique Values Only box so that an *X* appears.
   Figure III.4 shows the Query Properties dialog box.

3. Select OK.

To Use Crosstab Queries in Reports

To use a crosstab query in a report:

1. With the crosstab in Design view, set fixed columns headings
   (see *To Set Column Order* above). See *Design View* for more information about opening the crosstab in Design view.

2.   Click on the New Report button on the tool bar (illustrated on the inside back cover) and select Blank Report in the New Report dialog box.

3.   Click the Field List button in the tool bar (the fourth button from the left) or select View ➤ Field List.

4.   On the blank form, drag the fields from the query to the form.

5.   Add the additional fields you want (such as page number and report title).

6.   Save and/or run the report.

See Also   *Columns; Grids; Queries*

CURRENT RECORD INDICATORS

There are four indicators in Datasheet view that signify the status of a record.

   Indicates the current record

   Indicates a new record

   Indicates the record you are editing

   Indicates that another user is working with this record

See Also   *Editing Data; Records*

CUSTOMIZING ACCESS

You can customize the way Access displays data, prints forms and reports, and the defaults it uses throughout the system.

To Customize Access Options

To set the options that work throughout all modules in Access:

1. Select View ➤ Options from the main menu. The Options dialog box, shown in Figure III.5, appears.

2. Select one of the categories of options you want to change. Select from General, Keyboard, Printing, Form & Report Design, Datasheet, Query Design, Macro Design, Module Design, Multiuser.

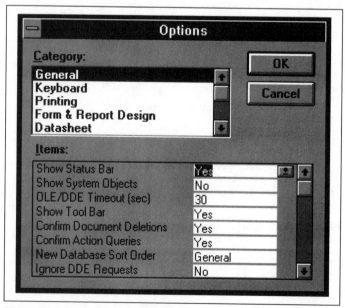

Figure III.5: The Options dialog box

3. Repeat step 2 for all the options you want to change.

4. Select OK.

● **NOTE** Module Design options refer to Access Basic Code, which is not covered in this book.

Custom Access Options: Datasheet

The following options and settings can be changed by selecting the Datasheet option in step 2 of *To Customize Access Options* above.

Option	Option controls	Valid settings
Default Column Width	Sets the width of columns	0 to 22 inches, 0 to 55.87 cm, or 0 to 31680 twips (a *twip* is $1/20$ of a point)
Default Font Italic	Sets whether to display the text with italics	Yes or No
Default Font Name	Sets the font to be used to display the datasheet	Select from installed Windows fonts.
Default Font Size	Sets the size of the font to be used to display the datasheet	Depends on the Windows fonts installed. You can enter any size from 1 to 127.
Default Font Underline	Sets whether to display the text with underlines	Yes or No
Default Font Weight	Sets the weight (thickness) of the font to be used to display the datasheet	Thin, Extra Light, Light, Normal, Medium, Semi-bold, Bold, Extra Bold, Heavy
Default Gridlines Behavior	Displays or hides the gridlines	On or Off

● **TIP**   Access does not provide a list of fonts to select from; you must know the font name and enter it in the font name text box.

● **TIP**   While you can enter any size from 1 to 127 as default font sizes in Access, very small and very large sizes are not useful.

Custom Access Options: Form and Report Design

The following options and settings can be changed by selecting the Form and Report Design option in step 2 of *To Customize Access Options* above.

Option	Option controls	Valid settings
Form Template	Specifies the form to use as a template when creating new forms with the FormWizard	Name of any form in the database
Report Template	Specifies the report to use as a template when creating new reports with the ReportWizard	Name of any report in the database
Objects Snap to Grid	Specifies whether controls should automatically align to grids during Design view when controls are added or moved	Yes or No
Selection Behavior	Specifies whether, when you use a mouse to draw a rectangle over controls, only those controls fully or partially inside the rectangle are selected	Partially Enclosed or Fully Enclosed

Option	Option controls	Valid settings
Show Grid	Whether Access should display grids automatically in a form or report's Design view	Yes or No
Show Ruler	Whether Access should display a ruler in a form or report's Design view	Yes or No

Custom Access Options: General

The following options and settings can be changed by selecting the General option in step 2 of *To Customize Access Options* above.

Option	Option controls	Valid settings
Confirm Action Queries	Prompts Access to ask you to confirm your request to run an action query	Yes or No
Confirm Document Deletions	Prompts Access to ask if you are sure you want to delete an object	Yes or No
Confirm Record Changes	Prompts Access to ask you to confirm your action when you delete records, paste records, or make changes to records using the Replace command	Yes or No

Option	Option controls	Valid settings
Default Database Directory	Drive and directory that contain the location of databases	Pathname. (A period [.] indicates Access should use the working directory defined in the Program Properties in the Windows Program Manager)
Default Find/Replace Behavior	Determines whether Access should search the current field and match a string on the entire field (Fast Search) or search all fields and match a string on any part of the field (General Search)	Fast Search or General Search
Ignore DDE Requests	Determines whether Access should honor or ignore DDE requests from other Windows applications	Yes or No

Option	Option controls	Valid settings
New Database Sort Order	Sets the sort order for sort operations on a database for new databases; to change the sort order on an existing database, you must change the setting, then compact the database	General, Traditional, Spanish, Dutch, or Nordic (see the Microsoft Access User Guide for a chart showing the sort order by ASCII character)
OLE/DDE Timeout	Sets the number of seconds between attempts if an unsuccessful OLE or DDE operation is encountered	0 to 300 seconds
Show Status Bar	Displays or hides the status bar	Yes or No
Show System Objects	Displays or hides the names of forms, reports, and other system objects from the Database window	Yes or No
Show Tool Bar	Displays or hides the tool bar at the top of all screens	Yes or No

Custom Access Options: Keyboard

The following options and settings can be changed by selecting the Keyboard option in step 2 of *To Customize Access Options* above.

Option	Option controls	Valid settings
Arrow Key Behavior	Whether arrow key should move to the next/previous field or next/previous character	Next Field or Next Character
Cursor Stops at First/Last Field	Whether pressing the arrow keys moves the insertion point past the first or last field in a row so that it can or cannot move to the previous (or next) record in the row above (or below)	Yes or No
Key Assignment Macro	Sets the name of the macro that controls the Key Assignment special macro	Any macro name
Move After Enter	Whether Enter moves the insertion point, and if so, whether the insertion point moves to the next field or the next record	No, Next Field, or Next Record

See Also *Using the Keyboard in Access* in Part II

Custom Access Options: Macro Design

The following options and settings can be changed by selecting the Macro Design option in step 2 of *To Customize Access Options* above.

Option	Option controls	Valid settings
Show Conditions Column	Displays or hides the Conditions column when you create new macros	Yes or No

Option	Option controls	Valid settings
Show Macro Names Column	Displays or hides the Macro Names column when you create new macros	Yes or No

See Also   *Macros*

Custom Access Options: Multiuser

The following options and settings can be changed by selecting the Multiuser option in step 2 of *To Customize Access Options* above.

Option	Option controls	Valid settings
Default Open Mode for Databases	Access mode of databases (how databases are shared)	Exclusive or Shared
Default Record Locking	How Access should lock records	No Locks, All Records, or Edited Records
Number of Update Retries	Number of times Access tried to save a record if that record is in use (locked) by another user	0 to 10
ODBC Refresh Interval	Number of seconds between attempts to refresh records read using ODBC	1 to 3600
Refresh Interval	Number of seconds between refreshes of records displayed on the screen	1 to 32,766 seconds

Option	Option controls	Valid settings
Update Retry Interval	Number of milliseconds between attempts to save a changed record in use by another user	0 to 1000

- **NOTE**   Open Database Connectivity (ODBC) allows you to add drivers so you can use a variety of database formats not directly supported by the basic Access system.

Custom Access Options: Printing

The following options and settings can be changed by selecting the Printing option in step 2 of *To Customize Access Options* above.

Option	Option controls	Valid settings
Bottom Margin	Size of the bottom margin	0 to height of a page
Left Margin	Size of left margin	0 to width of a page
Right Margin	Size of the right margin	0 to width of a page
Top Margin	Size of the top margin	0 to length of a page

See Also   *Printing*

Custom Access Options: Query Design

The following options and settings can be changed by selecting the Query Design option in step 2 of *To Customize Access Options* above.

Option	What option controls	Valid settings
Restrict Available Fields	Whether a field list for a new query displays all fields in the underlying table or only those selected in the QBE grid	Yes or No
Run with Owner's Permissions	Permission to view data in a query or run an action query (applies only to a multiuser, secure environment)	Yes or No
Show Table Names	Display or hide the table names row in the QBE grid	Yes or No

See Also   *Queries*

DAMAGED DATABASE

If an Access database becomes corrupted because of a hardware problem, such as an interruption in power or a problem with a hard disk, you may be able to recover the data.

To Recover a Damaged Database

To recover data from a database damaged due to unexpected conditions.

1. Close the database if it is open. The database must be closed by *all* users in a multiuser environment. Access's screen displays two menu options: File and Help. The rest of the window is empty.

2. Select File ➤ Repair Database from the main menu.

3. Select the file name of the database you want to repair. Database files have the extension .MDB.

4.   Access displays a progress indicator in the status bar at the bottom of the window.

DATA TYPES

Each field in a table contains a different type of data: text, dates, or numbers, for example. When creating or modifying a field in a table, select from one of these types.

Type	Can Contain	Limits
Counter	Number	Automatically assigned by Access to the next higher value in the table. Limit of value: 2,147,483,647.
Currency	Numbers representing money	Up to 15 digits to the left of the decimal point and 4 digits to the right
Date/Time	Dates and times	Only valid dates and times are allowed
Memo	Numbers and letters	32,000 characters (including spaces)
Number	Numbers, including those with decimals	See FieldSize property
OLE Object	Any object that provides an embed-dable or linkable object, such as a graphic, document, spreadsheet, or sound file	Object must be smaller than 128 MB
Text	Numbers and letters	255 characters (including spaces)

Type	Can Contain	Limits
Yes/No	Boolean values (true/false, yes/no, on/off)	Field may be contain only one of two values

● **TIP** The currency data type should be used in calculations in which you want to keep the number of digits fixed, and where precise calculations are required.

● **TIP** Though Access stores dates and times internally in only one way, you can display dates and times in a variety of formats. See *Formats* for more information.

See Also *Tables*

DATABASES

A database is a collection of tables, queries, forms, reports, macros, and modules (program code).

To Create a Database

1. Select File ➤ New Database from the main menu.
2. Enter the name of the new database in the File Name box. Database names must be legal DOS filenames: they are limited to 8 characters and numbers, and may not contain spaces. Access supplies the .MDB file extension.
3. Select the OK button in the New Database window.

To Open a Database

1. Select File ➤ Open Database from the main menu.

2. Select the drive, directory, and file name of the database you want to open.

3. Select OK. Access displays the Database window (see Figure A.1 in the Appendix).

To Open a Database in Shared Mode

In a multiuser environment, databases are usually placed on a network file server so that all users on the network have access to them.

To open a database in shared mode:

1. Select File ➤ Open Database from the main menu.

2. Select the drive, directory, and file name of the database you want to open.

3. If an *X* appears in the Exclusive check box, click on the box or press Alt-X to remove the *X*.

4. Select OK.

To Open a Database in Read-Only Mode

If you want to look at data in a database, but not change it, open the database in read-only mode. Read-only mode may also be required if you are working in a multiuser environment and another user needs exclusive use of the database.

To open a database in read-only mode:

1. Select File ➤ Open Database from the main menu.

2. Select the drive, directory, and file name of the database you want to open.

3. If an *X* does not appear in the Read Only box, click on the box or press Alt-R to add an *X*.

4. Select OK.

See Also   *Read-Only Files*

● **TIP** In most multiuser environments, you will want to set Exclusive to off —that is, not check the Exclusive option—if you select the Read Only option.

To Copy, Rename, or Delete a Database

To copy, rename, or delete a database within Access:

1. Close the database file. In a multiuser environment, all users must close the database.

2. Use the Windows File Manager or a third-party Windows utility program to perform the file operation. Databases have the .MDB file extension.

To Copy a Table to Another Database

To copy an existing table to another Access database:

1. Open the source database.

2. Highlight the table in the Database window.

3. Select Edit ➤ Copy.

4. Open the destination database.

5. Select Edit ➤ Paste from the main menu.

6. In the Paste Table As dialog box, enter the table's name.

7. Select whether you want to paste only the table's structure or whether you want to copy the structure and the data. You can also choose to append data to an existing database.

8. Select OK.

To Delete a Database

To delete a database:

1. Close the database. If you are running Access in a multiuser environment (on a network), be sure all users have closed the same database.

2.   Using the Windows File Manager or a third-party utility, delete the database file. Database files have the .MDB file extension.

● **NOTE**   You can also delete a database using the DOS **del** command at the DOS command line, or by using the Windows File Manager or a third-party file utility.

DATABASE WINDOW

The Database window (shown in Figure A.1 in the Appendix) is the main window that Access displays when you open a database.

DATASHEETS

Datasheets display data from tables and queries. To open a datasheet, click on the table or query that you want to run in the Database window and click on Open. A sample datasheet is shown in Figure A.6 in the Appendix.

To switch between Datasheet view and Design view, click on the Datasheet and Design buttons in the tool bar, or select View ➤ Datasheet or View ➤ Table Design (or View ➤ Query Design) from the main menu.

See Also   *Columns*

To Navigate within a Datasheet

The quick buttons for record access are in the bottom-left corner of the Datasheet window.

From the left to right:

	Moves to the first record in the table or query
	Moves to the previous record
	Moves to the next record
	Moves to the last record in the table or query

You can also press:

Tab	To move to the next field
Shift-Tab	To move to the previous field

In the middle of the navigation buttons is the record counter of the current record. Press F5 or click in the box then enter the record number you want to display and press Enter.

If there is more information than fits on a single screen Access displays scroll bars. Use the scroll bars to navigate around the datasheet.

You can move directly to the column of your choice by selecting the field from the Field list on the tool bar.

To limit the records displayed by a query's datasheet specify a filter. See *Filters* for more information.

See Also *Editing Data; Records*

To Close a Datasheet

When you have finished working with a datasheet and want to return to the Database window, select File ➤ Close.

You can also leave a datasheet by selecting another view using the tool bar—for example, select the Design button from the tool bar.

EDITING DATA AND RECORDS

Tables consist of records, which contain the actual data you want to keep.

To Add a Record Using a Datasheet

There are two ways to add data to a Datasheet:

1. Move to the bottom of the datasheet, to the record marked with an asterisk (*). You can move to this row by using the scroll bars or by selecting Records ➤ Go To/New from the main menu. This row is reserved for new data. When you begin to enter data in this row, Access inserts another row immediately below.

2. Select Records ➤ Data Entry from the main menu, or press Ctrl-+. Access displays a blank row. When you begin to enter data in this row, Access inserts another row immediately below.

● **TIP** If a default value has been defined for the field, press Ctrl-Alt-spacebar and the value is displayed.

When you want to insert the value from the previous record into the current field, press Ctrl-' (single quote).

See Also For more tips, see *Using the Keyboard in Access* in Part II.

To Find a Value in a Datasheet

To find a text string in one or more fields in a datasheet:

1. Click on the heading of the column containing the field you want to search. The entire column changes to reverse video.

2. Click on the Find button in the tool bar (it looks like a pair of binoculars; the tool bar is illustrated on the inside front cover)

3. Enter the value you want to find in the Find What box of the Find in field dialog box (see Figure III.6).

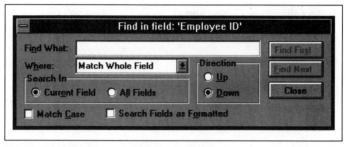

Figure III.6: The Find in field dialog box

4. Press Tab to move to the Where box. Click on the down-pointing arrow key, or press Alt-↓. Select Any Part of Field. This will find the value anywhere in the field, not just at the beginning of the field.

5. The Search In option box should be set to Current Field. (Select All Fields if you want to search two or more fields.) If it is not, click on the button to the left of the words *Current Field*.

6. If you are searching an entire column, you do not need to set the Direction value.

7. Select Find First.

8. Access displays the result of the search in reverse video.

9. To find the next occurrence of the value, select the Find Next button.

10. When you are done searching the field, select the Close button.

See Also   *Finding Data*

To Select Data in a Datasheet

To cut, copy, or paste fields or records, you must first select the data. Use these keyboard and mouse techniques to select data:

To select this	Keyboard	Mouse
Select a field	Press F2	Click at the beginning of the selection and drag the mouse to highlight the data, or click on the left edge of the cell
Select text within a field	Move the insertion point to the beginning of the field, then hold down Shift and move to the end of the selection	Click at the beginning of the selection and drag the mouse to highlight the data; or click at the beginning of the selection, then hold down Shift and click at the end of the selection
Select the current record	Press Shift-Spacebar	Click on the record selector (the small box at the leftmost edge of the window)
Select word within a field	Move the insertion point to the beginning of the word, then hold down Shift and move to the end of the word	Double-click anywhere in the word.

To select this	Keyboard	Mouse
Select more than one record	Press Shift-Spacebar, then hold down Shift and press ↑ or ↓ until all desired records are highlighted	Click on the record selector and drag the mouse pointer to the last record
Select all records	Select Edit ➤ Select all Records from the main menu	Click on the small record selector above all rows and to the left of column headings

To Copy or Move Data within a Datasheet

To copy or move data within the same datasheet:

1. Select the data you want to copy or move.

2. To copy the data, press Ctrl-C, or select Edit ➤ Copy from the main menu. To move the data, press Ctrl-X or select Edit ➤ Cut from the main menu.

3. Move the insertion point to the new location for the data.

4. Press Ctrl-V or select Edit ➤ Paste from the main menu.

To Copy or Move Records between Datasheets

You can copy or move records from one datasheet to another datasheet (including datasheets in other databases) *as long as the fields are in the same order.* If the selection you copy has more columns than the destination datasheet, the extra columns are not copied. If the selection has fewer columns, null values are used for the missing columns.

To copy or move records:

1. With the datasheet in Datasheet view, select the records you want to copy or move.

2. To copy the records, press Ctrl-C, or select Edit ➤ Copy from the main menu. To move the records, press Ctrl-X or select Edit ➤ Cut from the main menu.

3. Open the datasheet to receive the records. (If the columns are not in exactly the same order as the source columns, rearrange them now.)

4. To append records to the end of the datasheet, select Edit ➤ Paste Append from the main menu. If you want to replace records in this datasheet, select the records first, then press Ctrl-V or select Edit ➤ Paste from the main menu.

To Delete Data in a Datasheet

After selecting the data, press Del or select Edit ➤ Delete from the menu.

To Delete Records in a Datasheet

To remove records from a datasheet:

1. With the datasheet in Datasheet view, select the records you want to delete.

2. Press Ctrl-X or select Edit ➤ Cut from the main menu.

3. Access asks you to confirm the delete. Select OK to delete the records or Cancel to keep them.

DISPLAYING RECORDS IN A DATASHEET

This section describes how to change the way your data appears on the screen.

To Display the Most Current Information in a Datasheet

If you are making frequent updates to a table, or working in a multiuser environment, the data displayed in a datasheet may not be current. You have two options for updating the datasheet display:

Refreshing the records shows the most recent status, including which records were deleted, but does not show new records, change the order of the records, or change which record is current.

Requery displays new records and removes deleted records, so the order of records and the current record may change.

If you change a record's value so that it no longer meets the criteria of a query, specify Requery to remove it from the display.

To refresh the display, select Records, Refresh from the main menu.

To requery the database, press Shift-F9.

To Change Row Height

You can change the height of each row in a datasheet by using the mouse or the menus.

To change the row height using the mouse:

1. Move the pointer to the border of any row so that the pointer changes to a two-headed arrow with a bar through it.
2. Click and drag so that the row expands or contracts to the desired height, then Release the mouse button.

To change the row height using the menu:

1. Select Layout ➤ Row Height from the main menu.
2. Enter the desired row height in the Row Height box, or click on Standard Height to use the default height.
3. Select OK.

To Remove Gridlines

By default, datasheets are displayed with horizontal and vertical lines separating each row and column. To remove these *gridlines*, select Layout ➤ Gridlines from the main menu. This action works as a toggle: to turn the gridlines back on, select Layout ➤ Gridlines again.

DATES

Access tables can store date information. This section describes how you can enter and display dates in Access.

To Add the Current Date and Time

To add the current date and time to a form or report:

1. Open the form or report in Design view. See *Design View* for more information.

2. Add a text box to the appropriate area (section) of the form or report.

3. Click on the Properties button in the tool bar, or select View ➤ Properties.

4. Enter **=Date()** (for the current date) or **=Now()** (for the date and current time) in the Control Source property.

5. Set the Format property with a standard or custom format.

See Also   *Fields; Formats*

DATE FUNCTIONS

Access uses the following date functions:

Function	Purpose
CVDate (expression)	converts a date expression (for example, "July 25, 1995") to a serial date; serial dates are between – 657434 (January 1, 100 AD) to 2958465 (December 31, 9999 AD)
Date	Returns date with date stored as a double.

Function	Purpose
DatePart (period, date)	Returns the part of the date specified by period. Date can be a string expression that contains a date, or a Date/Time field. For period parameters, see the list below this one.
DateSerial (year, month, day)	Returns the serial date for the given year (0 through 9999), month (1 through 12), and day (1 through 31). Year, month, and day are numbers or numeric expressions.
DateValue (string)	Returns a date based on *string*. *String* holds the date in the format specified in the International portion of the WIN.INI file.
Date$	Returns date in the form mm-dd-yyyy (for example, 07-04-1995)
Day (serialdate)	Returns the day number (from 01 to 31) of the serial date.
IsDate (argument)	Returns true if the argument is a valid serial date or date expression.
Weekday (number)	Returns an integer representing the day of the week, from 1 (Sunday) through 7 (Saturday); number is a serial date or numeric expression.

Use the following strings for the DatePart period parameter:

d	day
h	hour
m	month
n	minute
q	quarter
s	second
w	weekday (01 is Sunday, 07 is Saturday)

ww	week number (01–52)
y	day of the year (01–366)
yyyy	year

DBASE

dBASE is an industry standard format for database data. Access can read and write dBASE data, making it easy to use data from a variety of other programs.

To Save Tables in dBASE Format

To create a copy of an Access table in dBASE format:

1. Close the table. If you are working in a multiuser environment, all users must close the table.

2. Open the Database window by pressing F11.

3. Select File ➤ Export from the main menu. Access displays the Export dialog box, shown in Figure III.7.

4. In the Data Destination text box, select the dBASE III or dBASE IV format, then select OK.

5. From the list of tables in the current database, select the table you want to export, then select OK.

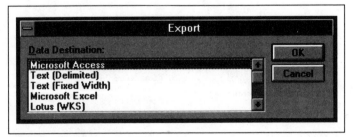

Figure III.7: The Export dialog box

6.   Enter the name of the file you want to export *to*. Access
adds the .DBF file extension for you if necessary.

7.   Access adjusts field names if they are too long or do not conform to dBASE standards (for example, if they contain spaces).

To Use dBASE Files

To attach or import a file from a dBASE database:

1.   Be sure an Access database is open.

2.   Select File ➤ Attach Table from the main menu to attach a
dBASE file. Select File ➤ Import to import a dBASE file.

3.   Select dBASE III or dBASE IV as the Data Source.

4.   Select the dBASE file you want to use. dBASE files have
the .DBF extension.

5.   If you *import* the file, Access creates the table automatically, and your task is complete. Repeat step 4 until you
have selected all needed files. Click on Close.

6.   If you *attach* the file, Access prompts you for the dBASE
index file name(s). Index files have the file extension .NDX
for single indexes and .MDX for files containing multiple
indexes. Select each index file you need. Click on Close
when you are done.

Access converts some dBASE data types to those Access can
use. Access performs the following conversions:

dBASE type	Access type (FieldSize Property)
Character	Text
Date	Date/Time
Float	Number (Double)
Memo	Memo
Numeric	Number (Double)

See Also   *Attach a Database; Import a Database; Export a Table*

DEFAULT PROPERTY

The *default property* is assigned to a command button on a form. It determines which button in a group will be pressed when the user presses the Enter key. The button with the default property appears emphasized.

DEFAULT VALUES

Setting a default value for fields speeds up data entry. During data entry, you can have Access fill in the default value for fields by pressing Ctrl-Alt-spacebar.

To Set a Default Value for a Field

To set the default value for a field, so that Access fills in the value when a new record is created:

1. Open the table in Design view. See *Design View* for more information.

2. Select the field you want to change by clicking on it.

3. In the Field Properties window at the bottom of the screen, select the Default Value property.

4. Enter the default value (an explicit value or expression) in the Default Value box. Enter **=Yes** or **=No** in Yes/No fields.

If you change a field's default value, existing data for the field is not changed.

See Also *Properties*

DESIGN VIEW

When you design an Access object such as a form, report, or query, you define the object's layout or properties. When your design is ready to be tested, you can switch to execution mode and test the object. For example, you can design a form in Design view, then switch to Form view, which displays the first record in the table or query using the form you have designed.

A sample form in Design view is shown in Figure A.8 in the Appendix. A sample report in Design view is shown in Figure A.12 in the Appendix.

To Switch between Design View and Execution Mode

You can switch between Design view or Form view and execution mode, which displays the result of your design, by using buttons on the tool bar or by using the menu.

Tool bar: Click on the Design View button to switch to Access' design mode. Click on the Run button in the tool bar (the button with the large exclamation point), or the second button from the left on the tool bar. This button's face changes depending on the object you are working on: For example, when you are working with a query, it shows a Datasheet, since this is the object used to display the results of a query.

Menus: Select View from the main menu. The pull-down list of menu options changes depending on the type of object you are working on. For example, if you are working with a query, the pull-down options are Query Design or Datasheet. Select Query Design to return to Design view, and select Datasheet to execute the query. Similarly, if you are working with a form, you can select View ➤ Form Design to move to Design view, View ➤ Form to see the data filled in on the form, or View ➤ Datasheet to view the data in a Datasheet.

To Modify an Object in Design View

To modify an object's design in Design view:

1. Open the Database window by pressing F11.

2. Select the button representing the type of object you want to modify: select the Table, Query, Form, Report, or Macro button.

3. Access displays a list of the objects of the type you selected. For example, if you selected Table in step 2, Access displays a list of all the existing tables.

4. Select the name of the object you want by pressing ↑ or ↓ until the name is highlighted, then select Design by clicking on the Design button at the top of the window (or by pressing Alt-D).

5. Access displays the object you selected in the appropriate design window. For example, if you selected a table, Access opens the Table Design window for that table.

See Also   *Forms; Reports*

DRAWING TOOLS

Lines and rectangles add visual clues to your form, helping you to group related elements, draw attention to important fields, or add interest to the form. Rectangles can surround existing form and report elements (fields).

To Draw Lines

To draw a line on a form or report:

1. Open the form or report in Design view. See *Design View* for more information.

2. Display the toolbox (select View ➤ Toolbox if the toolbox is not visible). The toolbox is illustrated on the inside front cover.

3. Select the line tool.

4. Click the mouse to display the first endpoint, drag to the other endpoint, and release the mouse button.

5. To change the line thickness or color, click on the palette button in the tool bar or select View ➤ Palette from the main menu. Select the color in the Border row and the line width in the Width row, and make sure that the Clear box does not have an X in it.

To Draw Rectangles

To draw a rectangle on a form or report:

1. Open the form or report in Design view. See *Design View* for more information.

2. Display the toolbox (select View ➤ Toolbox if the toolbox is not visible). The toolbox is illustrated on the inside front cover.

3. Select the rectangle tool from the tool box.

4. Click to display the first corner and drag to the opposite corner, then release the mouse button.

5. If the rectangle is drawn over existing controls, select Layout ➤ Send to Back from the main menu. The existing controls appear on top of the rectangle you have drawn.

6. To change the line thickness, color, or 3D appearance of the rectangle, click on the palette button in the tool bar or select View ➤ Palette from the main menu. Select the color in the Border row and the line width in the Width row, and select an appearance (use Raised or Sunken for a 3D effect). Be sure that the Clear box does not have an X in it.

To Modify Existing Objects

To delete an object, click on it. When the black squares that mark the corners of the object appear, press Del or select Edit ➤ Delete from the main menu.

To move an object, click on it and hold down the mouse button. When the black squares marking the corners appear, move the mouse until a solid black hand appears. Drag the object to its new location.

To change the size of an object, click on it. To stretch or shrink the drawing's size and shape, click on and drag any of the black boxes that appear.

DYNASET

A dynaset is a set of records resulting from a query or filter. When you edit records in a dynaset, you are actually editing the records in the original tables. Unlike some database programs that create a separate table as the result of a query or filter, Access's dynasets are simply a subset of the actual, live records in the original table, so you must be careful when editing data—you are working with the *actual* data. Changes you make in the dynaset are made to the original record, *not* a copy.

EDITING DATA

Once you have entered data in Access, you'll need to update it. This section gives you directions for doing so.

To Change a Cell Value

The following options work in the grids Access uses throughout the system. For example, you can change a cell value in the Property window, a Datasheet view, or Query grid.

You can change a value in a cell in one of three ways.

- Enter the value you want directly in the cell. For example, enter some text, or **Yes/No**.

- Click on the down-pointing arrow, or press Alt-↓ to display a list of options. Use ↑ and ↓ to highlight the option you want, then press Enter.

- Many cells are restricted to a set of values, such as Yes/No. Click on the down-pointing arrow, or press Alt-↓ to display a list of options. Click directly on the option name.

See Also   *Queries*

EMBEDDING AND LINKING OBJECTS

You can store other documents (word-processing documents, bitmaps, graphics, spreadsheets, and even sounds) in a field in a table if the field has an OLE Object data type. The objects themselves (the spreadsheet or graphic, for example) are created in other Windows applications that support Object Linking and Embedding (OLE).

With OLE, when you display a record containing a field of the OLE Object data type and double-click on the field, Windows automatically launches the application that created the object. Furthermore, you can edit the object in the application that created it, then save it and update the object in the field in the Access table.

EMBEDDING OBJECTS IN FORMS AND REPORTS

The following instructions are used to create new unbound objects on forms and reports. These objects are constant; they do not change when a different record is displayed, for example. If the object is a Windows Paintbrush file, the unbound control will display the same image on each form and page of the report.

Objects such as the Windows Paintbrush image can be *embedded* into an unbound control on the form or report or *linked* into an unbound control on a form or report.

- If the source is embedded, the object is stored within the Access database.

- If the object source is linked, changes to the object can be made in another program (such as Windows Paintbrush); when changes are made, Access will use the newest version.

Since linked files are saved outside of Access (that is, the linked objects are kept in a separate file), they can be used in more than one Windows application; changes to the object will be reflected in all Windows applications linked to the object.

To Add and *Embed* an Unbound Object in a Form or Report

These instructions will create a new object on a form or report, launch the application you specify and let you create the object, then return you to the form or report and embed the newly created object. You can also insert a graphic image from an existing file.

1. Select the form or report you want to modify and open it in Design view. See *Design View* for more information.

2. Select the unbound object frame button from the toolbox. The toolbox is illustrated on the inside front cover.

3. Move the mouse to the form. Click the upper-left corner of the control, and drag to the bottom-right corner. Release the mouse button.

4. Access displays the Insert Object dialog box, shown in Figure III.8. The list of object types will depend on the OLE-compatible applications you've installed.

5. To insert a graphic image from an existing file, select File. The File dialog box appears. Select the file you want, then select OK and skip to step 7.

6. If the image you want to insert is from an OLE-compatible application, you can create the image in that application. Select the type of object you want to embed. When you select OK, Windows launches that application (the *OLE server*). When you have finished creating the image, select File ➤ Exit or File ➤ Exit and Return (or a similar file menu option). The OLE server asks if you want to update the object you just created in Access. Select Yes.

7. Access embeds the object in a control on the form. You can modify the control—you can resize and reshape it, for example.

The object is saved as part of the form. For example, if the object was created in Windows Paintbrush, there is no separate .PCX file: All the information about the image is stored within the Access form or report itself. To edit the image, open the form or report in Design view and double-click the image. Windows will launch the application that created the image, allow you to edit the object, then return you to Access, where the new version of the object can be stored.

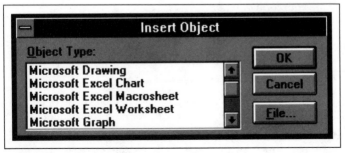

Figure III.8: The Insert Object dialog box.

To Add and *Link* an Unbound Object to a Form or Report

A linked object is saved as a separate file in the application that created it. When you use a linked object, Access does not save the object within the database: The object is maintained as a file outside Access. Using a linked file rather than an embedded file allows you to create a logo or other graphic object and share it in several Windows applications. When you modify the image in Paintbrush, all applications that have links to the object will automatically use the new version of the graphic file.

With these instructions, you first start in the application that created the object, copy the object to the Clipboard, and paste the object into an unbound control on a form or report. The object is stored in a separate file and is not part of Access. You tell Access that when this object is changed (when a new version is saved to your hard disk, for example), Access will display the new version of the object.

The following instructions assume the object you want to link to your form or report has already been created. If not, first create the object and save it as a separate file.

1. Open the application used to create the object, such as Windows Paintbrush. If the object can be used by more than one application, such as a standard graphics file in Windows Paintbrush format, you can use any application that supports (opens) the object's file format.

2. Open the file containing the object you want to link to your form or report.

3. Copy the object to the Clipboard. In most Windows applications, you must select the object, then select Edit ➤ Copy from the application's main menu.

4. Switch to Microsoft Access.

5. Select the form or report you want to modify and open it in Design view. See *Design View* for more information.

6. Select Edit ➤ Paste Link from the main menu. Access displays the Paste Link dialog box, shown in Figure III.9.

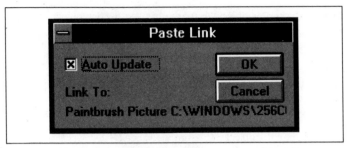

Figure III.9: The Paste Link dialog box.

7. If you want Access to automatically refresh the link when it opens the form or report, check the Auto Update check box. When this option is selected, Access will automatically read the file containing the source object whenever it changes. Auto Update ensures that you always have the most up-to-date copy of the source object.

- If you select Manual Link, you must use the menu system to update the link explicitly. For example, if you change the graphic object in Paintbrush and save the file, Access will not automatically repaint the image in your unbound control if the Manual Link option is set. Instead, you must select the object to update, then select Edit from the main menu, select the appropriate entry for the object from the pull-down menu (e.g. *Paintbrush picture object*), then select the Update Now menu option.

8. Select OK.

9. Access adds an unbound object frame to the form or report. You can now move, resize, and modify the object.

To Prevent an Object on a Form or Report from Being Edited

If you have an embedded or linked object on a form and want to temporarily or permanently stop the embedded or linked object from being changed, perform the following steps. These instructions are useful for graphic objects, but are not used for text objects, such as word-processing documents or spreadsheets, because converting text-based objects to pictures does not make sense.

Note that this procedure does not delete the object from the form or report: It only breaks the link to prevent editing. To delete the object, delete it as you would any other control—select it in Design view, then press Del or select Edit ➤ Cut from the main menu.

1. Open the object in Design view. See *Design View* for more information.

2. Select Edit from the main menu. From the pull-down menu, select the menu option that reflects the type of object you have (for example: *Microsoft Graph Object*).

3. Select Change to Picture.

EMBEDDING OBJECTS IN FIELDS

If you have a field in your table that is an OLE Object data type, these instructions show you how to embed an object into the field. Each record can contain a different object.

If you are using a form to update an OLE Object field, these instructions assume that you have added a bound object frame to the form.

To *Embed* an Object in a Record

Follow these instructions to embed an OLE object in a field in an Access table.

1. Open a form in Form view. If you are working with a query or datasheet, be sure you are in Datasheet view, not Design view. See *Design View* for more information.

2. Move to the record that is to contain the OLE object.

3. Select the field (in a datasheet) or the bound object frame (in a form) that will store the object.

4. Select Edit ➤ Insert Object from the main menu.

5. Access displays the Insert Object dialog box and asks for the type of OLE object you want. Only objects listed in this box can be embedded in the field. Select the object and select OK.

6. Windows opens the source application. Create the object you want to embed, or open an existing object using the source application's File ➤ Open menu commands. When you are done creating or editing the object, select File ➤ Exit and Return or File ➤ Update from the source application's main menu.

7. If the source application asks if you want to update the object, select Yes.

When you display the record, you can double-click on the object and Windows automatically opens the source application, displays the object in that application, and allows you to edit the object.

To *Embed* an Existing File in a Record

These instructions let you embed an OLE object in a field in an Access table.

1. Open a form in Form view. If you are working with a query or datasheet, be sure you are in Datasheet view, not Design view. See *Design View* for more information.

2. Move to the record that is to contain the OLE object.

3. Select the field (in a datasheet) or the bound object frame (in a form) that will store the object.

4. Select Edit ➤ Insert Object from the main menu.

5. Access displays the Insert Object dialog box and asks for the type of OLE object you want. Only objects listed in this box can be embedded in the field. Select the type of object, then select the File button.

6. Windows opens the Insert Objects from File dialog box.

   • Select the drive containing the file you want to embed.

- Select the directory containing the file you want to embed.

- Select the name of the file you want to embed in the Access table's field.

- Select OK.

7.   If you are in Form view, Access displays the object. If you are in Datasheet view, Access shows the type of object in the cell.

To *Link* an Object in a Record

These instructions let you link an existing object (saved in a disk file) in an OLE object field of an Access table. They assume the object you want to link to the field has already been created. If not, create the object and save it as a separate file.

1.   Open the application used to create the object, for example Windows Paintbrush. If the object can be used by more than one application, such as a standard graphics file in Windows Paintbrush format, you can use any application that supports (opens) the object's file format.

2.   Open the file containing the object you want to link to your field.

3.   Copy the object to the Clipboard. In most Windows applications, you must select the object, then select Edit ➤ Copy from the application's main menu.

4.   Switch to Microsoft Access.

5.   Open a form in Form view or Datasheet view, or open a table or query in Datasheet view. The form, query, or table must contain the table that contains the OLE object field you want linked to the source you saved in step 3.

6.   Move to the record that you want to modify.

7.   Select the OLE object field in the form or datasheet by clicking on it or by pressing Tab until the field is selected.

8.   Select Edit ➤ Paste Link from the main menu. Access displays the Paste Link dialog box. Select OK.

9.   In Form view, Access displays the object. In Datasheet
view, Access displays the type of object you have linked.

To Make an OLE Object Uneditable

If you want to break the link so that the contents of an OLE object
can no longer be edited or changed, follow these instructions. These
instructions are useful for graphic objects, but are not used for
sound or text objects, such as word-processing documents or
spreadsheets, because converting text-based objects to pictures
does not make sense, and does not work for sound objects.

Note that this procedure does not delete the object from the field—
it only breaks the link to prevent editing. To delete the contents of
the field (that is, to remove the object from the field), delete it as you
would any other field value—select the field, then press Del or
select Edit ➤ Cut from the main menu.

1.   Open a form in Form view. If you are working with a
query or datasheet, be sure you are in Datasheet view, not
Design view. See *Design View* for more information.

2.   Select Edit from the main menu. From the pull-down
menu, select the menu option that reflects the type of
object you have (for example: Microsoft Graph Object).

3.   Select Change to Picture.

See Also   *Forms; Reports; Graphics; Controls*

ENCRYPT OR DECRYPT A DATABASE

When you encrypt a database, Access compacts the database and
make it difficult, if not impossible, for a user with a file-browsing
utility to view the contents of the database. Encryption does not
restrict database access.

See Also See *Passwords* and *User and Group Accounts* for methods of controlling access to data.

To Encrypt or Decrypt a Database

To encrypt an unencrypted database, or decrypt an encrypted database:

1. Close the Database window if it is open. Access' screen displays two menu options: File and Help. The rest of the window is empty.

2. From the main menu select File ➤ Encrypt/Decrypt Database.

3. Select the database you want to encrypt or decrypt, then select OK. Access examines the database and decides which operation (encrypt or decrypt) you want.

4. Enter the name of the new, encrypted (or decrypted) database, or enter the current database name to replace the existing database with an encrypted version, in the Encrypt Database As (or Decrypt Database As) field.

EXPORT A TABLE

Exporting a table allows you to use Access data in another application.

To Export a Table

To create a copy of an Access table in another file format:

1. Close the table. If you are working in a multiuser environment, all users must close the table.

2. Open the Database window by pressing F11.

3. Select File ➤ Export from the main menu.

4. In the Data Destination text box, select the type of file format you want to use, then select OK.

5. From the list of tables in the current database, select the table you want to export, then select OK.

6. Enter the name of the file you want to export *to*. Access adds the proper file extension for you.

7. Access may ask you for further options, depending on the type of file format you are using. For example, in exporting to a delimited text field, Access asks if you want to store the field name in the first row (first record).

8. Access asks for a destination file name in the Export to File dialog box. Supply one.

9. Access adjusts field names if they are too long or do not conform to the output file format's standards.

See Also For specific information about database formats, see *Btrieve*, *dBASE*, *FoxPro*, *Paradox*, or *SQL Databases*.

EXPRESSIONS

Expressions are used to specify criteria in queries, perform updates in an action query (to multiply a field by 110%, for example), and in reports.

Expressions consist of fields in a table called identifiers (for example, Price or Quantity), literals (the value 1000 or "Seattle"), functions (such as Average or Sum), operators (such as * for multiplication), and constants (such as 1.05 and Yes).

Literals are typically text strings which can vary. Constants are values (text, numeric, data, etc.) that remain stable or are rarely changed, such as a tax rate, discount rate, or fiscal year begin date.

Expressions can be used:

- to compute the value of a calculated field; expressions are stored in the Control Source property of a control on a form or report;

- in validation expressions, to compare the value of a field entry with a calculated value; expressions are used in the Validation Rule property of such controls;

- to compute the default value of a control; expressions are used in the DefaultValue property of such controls; or

- in queries and filters, to select subsets of records based on a value calculated using other fields, or to update fields in the same record (in Action Queries).

There are several parts to the field reference used in expressions. You surround the name of the form, report, field, control, and property with square brackets. For example, in an expression you must refer to the field Price as [Price], as in **=[Price] * [Quantity]**.

Separator characters are also used to isolate the names of objects. The exclamation point (!) is used to separate the names of forms, reports, controls, and fields, such as **Forms!MyForm**.

The dot (.) typically separates a property from the rest of the identifier, and is used to separate a method when using Access Basic code. Access may also require you to use the words *Forms*, *Reports*, or *Screen* when you refer to a field on a form, report, or screen that is not active. This qualifier is necessary to avoid confusion. For example: **Forms!Myform!Visible**

When you create an expression:

- enclose object names (the names of fields, tables, queries, forms, reports, and controls) in square brackets; for example: **[First Name]**

- put number signs (#) around dates; for example: **#7/1/94#**

- put double-quotation marks (") around text; for example: **"New Jersey"**

To Use an Expression—Examples

To refer to the field named Price on the Inventory form when the Inventory form is not currently the active form, use the identifier **Forms![Inventory]![Price]** in a calculation. To refer to the default value of the same field when the Inventory form is active, use the identifier **[Price].[DefaultValue]** in a calculation.

EXPRESSION FUNCTIONS

The following functions can be used in a calculation. n is any number or numeric expression

Function Syntax	What function calculates
Abs (number)	absolute value of a number; e.g., Abs (–5) = 5
Atn (n)	arctangent of n expressed in radians
Cos (n)	cosine of n, where n is measured in radians
Exp (number)	e raised to a power, where e is the base of natural logarithms
Fix (n)	the integer part of n, a number or numeric expression; e.g., Fix (2.4) returns 2. When n is negative, fix returns the next *larger* integer; e.g., Fix (-5.6) returns –5. Compare with Int (n).
Int (n)	the integer part of n, a number or numeric expression; e.g., Int (2.7) returns 2. When n is negative, int returns the next *smaller* integer; e.g., Int (-5.6) returns –6. Compare with Fix (n).
Log (n)	the natural logarithm of n

Function Syntax	What function calculates
Rnd (n)	a pseudo-random number. If n is less than 0, Rnd (n) returns the same value after every call. If n is zero, Rnd (n) returns the last generated number. If n is greater than 0 or omitted, Rnd returns the next pseudo-randomly–generated number.
Sgn (n)	the sign of a n. Sgn returns 1 if n is greater than 0; it returns 0 when n is 0; and −1 when n is negative.
Sin (n)	the sine of n, where n is measured in radians
Sqrt (n)	the square root of n, returned as a number of data type double
Sum ([FieldName])	sum of all values in FieldName of a dynaset
Tan (n)	tangent of n, where n is measured in radians

ARITHMETIC OPERATORS

Access uses the following arithmetic operators:

&	concatenates two text strings; e.g., [City] & " " & [State] would return a single text field consisting of the value in the City field, a space, and the value in the State field
+	adds two numbers or numeric expressions; e.g., [Sub Total] + [Tax Amount]
−	subtracts two numbers or numeric expressions (e.g., [Stock On Hand] - [Amt Ordered]) -or- reverses the sign of a field (e.g., −[Price])
*	multiplies two numbers or numeric expressions; e.g., [Sub Total] * [Tax Rate]
/	divides two numbers or numeric expressions; e.g., [Sales Amt] / [Total Sales]

\	divides two numbers or numeric expressions and returns an integer or long value
mod	divides two numbers or numeric expressions and returns the remainder only
^	raise a number of a power; e.g., 10^2 equals 10 to the second power, the result of 10^2 is 100

LOGICAL OPERATORS

Logical operators can be used on either Boolean (Yes/No) data or numeric data. When they are used with numeric data, they perform bitwise logical operations.

Operator	What it performs
and	logical conjunction of two expressions (both expressions must be true for the expression as a whole to be true)
eqv	logical equivalence of two expressions
imp	logical implication of two expressions
not	logical opposite of an expression (if the expression preceding *not* is false, the expression as a whole is true)
or	logical disjunction of two expressions (if either expression is true, the complete expression is true)
xor	logical exclusive or of two expressions

See the lists below for further exposition of these logical operators.

AND Operator

Expression1	Expression2	Result
true	true	true
true	false	false
true	null	null

Expression1	Expression2	Result
false	true	false
false	null	false
null	true	null
null	false	false
null	null	null

EQV Operator

Expression1	Expression2	Result
true	true	true
true	false	false
true	null	null
false	true	false
false	false	true
false	null	null
null	true	null
null	false	null
null	null	null

IMP Operator

Expression1	Expression2	Result
true	true	true
true	false	false
true	null	null
false	true	true
false	false	true
false	null	true

Expression1	Expression2	Result
null	true	true
null	false	null
null	null	null

NOT Operator

Expression	Result
true	false
false	true
null	null

OR Operator

Expression1	Expression2	Result
true	true	true
true	false	true
true	null	true
false	true	true
false	false	false
false	null	null
null	true	true
null	false	null
null	null	null

XOR Operator

Expression1	Expression2	Result
true	true	false
true	false	true

Expression1	Expression2	Result
true	null	null
false	true	true
false	false	false
false	null	null
null	true	null
null	false	null
null	null	null

EXPRESSIONS IN QUERIES

When specifying a criteria in a query window, use an expression to limit the records Access finds or displays. Expressions need an object name or value and an operator.

Operator	Meaning	Example Criteria
=	equals	= "New Jersey"
<	less than	< 100
<=	less than or equal to	<= 100
>	greater than	> #7/1/94#
>=	greater than or equal to	>= 21
<>	Not equal to	<> "Seattle"

THE IN OPERATOR

The In operator is used to specify a set of values a field value must match. For example, to specify in a query that the State field contain WA, ID, or CA, the criteria in the QBE grid should be **In("WA", "ID", "CA")**.

The In operator lets you specify several or conditions on a single line. The example above is equivalent to saying the State field must contain WA or ID or CA.

To *exclude* records that match the values in the list, use the Not operator. For example, to exclude records from the three states, the criteria in the QBE grid of a query should be **Not In("WA", "ID", "CA")**.

THE LIKE OPERATOR

The Like operator is used to compare a Text or Date/Time field with a string expression. The Like operator uses a pattern which contains wildcard operators (listed below). For example, the expression [Last Name] Like "B*" matches all last names that begin with the letter B and contain zero or more characters following the B. In a query, the expression Like "B*" is entered in the Criteria row for the [Last Name] field.

The pattern can contain any of the following wildcard characters:

*	Zero or more characters; examples: the pattern "C*" matches fields containing "Cash" and "credit" but not "money"; 1/*/95 matches all dates in January 1995
?	A single character; examples: the pattern "B?T" matches fields containing "bat" and "bit" but not "brat"; 1/1?/95 matches all dates from 1/10/95 through 1/19/95
#	A single number (0 through 9); e.g., "##" matches "01" and "99" but not "A1"
[charlist]	match any character in the charlist (e.g., [a-z] matches only letters); characters must be in ascending order: a–z, then A–Z, then 0–9
[!charlist]	matches any character *not* in the charlist (e.g., [!a-z] matches strings that do not contain letters)

● **TIP**   If the entry area for your expression is too small, press Shift-F2 to open the Zoom window. Enter your expression, then press OK to return to the Property window.

See Also   *Validating Data; Queries; Filters*

FIELDS

You can work with fields in a table that is displayed in Design view. A Table window displaying the fields in the sample Employees table is shown in Figure A.3 in Appendix.

To Add Fields to a Table

To add fields to an existing Access table:

1. Enter the name of the field (up to 64 characters, including spaces and special characters, but not including periods, exclamation points, and square brackets) in the first blank field in the Field Name column.

2. Select the type of data to be stored in the field. In the Data Type column, enter the type name, or click on the down-pointing arrow key and select from the list. See *Data Types* for more information.

3. Enter a description for the field. The description allows you to describe in more detail the purpose of the field, or information about the source of the data. The description is for reference only and is not used within Access when performing tasks or operations.

4. Enter field properties in the area below the field names. Click on any field property, or press F6 to jump between areas.

To Use Field Properties

Field properties determine how data is saved and displayed, and are different for each data type (text, date, number, and so on). Field properties are set in the lower half of the window used to design a Table.

Enter the property value on the corresponding line in the Field Properties window.

The following field properties are available:

FieldSize | Determines the length of a text field or the type of number to be stored; see below

Format | Determines how data is displayed. Access has predefined formats and you can create your own custom formats

DecimalPlaces | The number of digits to the right of the decimal in numeric fields

Caption | The field label used by default in forms and reports

DefaultValue | The value to be saved in the field of a new record if no entry is made in the field

ValidationRule | The formula or rule that must be satisfied before the value will be saved in the field

ValidationText | The text that is displayed on the screen if the ValidationRule fails

Indexed | Whether or not the field is used as an index field. Indexes speed up searching and sorting. See Indexes in this guide for more information

● **TIP**   DefaultValues are useful when the majority of your records have the same value. For example, if most parts are ordered singly, an Order Quantity field's DefaultValue can be set to 1. The number 1 appears in the Order Quantity field automatically when you are adding new records in a form.

● **TIP**   Use *Is not null* as the ValidationRule to require an entry in the field during data entry.

To Set Field Size

The FieldSize property is set in Table Design view. It determines the amount of space reserved for fields with a Numeric or Text data type.

For text fields, enter the maximum number of characters the field can contain. The largest text field size is 255 characters.

For numbers, the FieldSize property determines the length of a number, and thus its minimum and maximum values. Valid settings for a Number data type are listed from smallest to largest.

Property	Field can contain	Bytes used
Byte	Whole numbers from 0–255	1
Integer	Whole numbers from –32,768 to 32,767	2
Long Integer	Whole numbers from –2,147,483,648 to 2,147,483,647	4
Single	Numbers (including fractional parts), from –3.402823E38 to 3.402823E38. (E38 represents 10 to the 38th power) Numbers are accurate to 6 decimal digits.	4
Double	Numbers (including fractional parts) from –1.79769313486232E308 to 1.79769313486232E308. Numbers are accurate to 10 decimal digits.	8

• **NOTE**   A *byte* is the amount of space needed to store a single character, such as *A*.

To Insert Fields in a Table

To insert a field in a table, select the row (move the insertion point to the row or click the mouse in the row) in which you want the new field placed. The field already in this row and all fields in rows underneath below is shifted down one row. Select Edit ➤ Insert Row.

DELETING FIELDS FROM A TABLE

To delete a field in a table, select the row (move the insertion point to the row or click in the row) and select Edit ➤ Delete Row.

To delete multiple rows, place the pointer in the row of the first Field Name you want to remove. The pointer changes to a horizontal arrow. Drag down to the last row you want to delete. Each row appears highlighted. Press Delete or select Edit ➤ Delete Row.

To delete all rows, select Edit ➤ Select All from the main menu. Press Delete or select Edit ➤ Delete Row.

To Move Fields in a Table

Move the pointer to the row containing the field you want to move. When the pointer changes to a horizontal, solid arrow, click the mouse. The current record pointer (in the leftmost column) changes to a left-pointing triangle and the row is highlighted. Drag the triangle to the new row and release the mouse button.

To Change Field Types

To change the data type of a field:

1. Open a table in Design view. See *Design View* for more information.

2. Select the Data Type of the field you want to change.

3. Select the new data type. (You cannot select a Counter data type.)

4. Select File ➤ Save from the main menu.

5. To stop the conversion, press Ctrl-Break.

When converting from larger field sizes to smaller, Access truncates the value. For example, if you convert from a memo to a text field of 40 characters, only the first 40 characters in the memo field will be converted. If you convert from a larger numeric field to a smaller one, Access will make the conversion unless the value will not fit in the new field, in which case no conversion is made.

When you convert from text to numeric, Access interprets the separator characters (period and comma) to interpret the numeric value. When you convert from a numeric or date field to a text field, Access displays the number using the General number or date format.

If Access cannot convert a value from the old data type to the new data type, it leaves the new value blank. Access warns you and allows you to stop this from happening.

If the field whose data type you have changed is an index field or primary key for a table *and* if Access cannot convert a value or the converted value is not unique in the table, Access deletes the entire record. Access warns you and allows you to stop this from happening.

See Also   *Primary key*

FILTERS

Filters allow you to set criteria and display the results on a form. Unlike queries, you cannot save a filter's settings for reuse. Filters display all records at once, unlike a Find, which displays records one at a time.

As with queries, the Access table still contains all the records it had before you applied the filter. Additionally, you can modify the records displayed in a filter, just as you can in a query.

To Create or Modify a Filter

To find a subset of records in the table, set a filter as follows:

1. Open a form in Design view or Datasheet view. See *Design View* or *Datasheet* for more information.

2. Click on the Edit Filter/Sort button in the tool bar (the first button after "Filter/Sort" in the tool bar, illustrated on the inside front cover), or select Records ➤ Edit Filter/Sort from the main menu. Access displays the Filter window shown in Figure A.10 in the Appendix.

3. Enter the field name or drag the field name from the table window at the top of the Filter window to the Field row in the grid at the bottom of the Filter window.

4. Enter the criteria and sort order.

5. Click on the Apply Filter/Sort button in the tool bar (the second button after Filter/Sort in the tool bar), or select Records ➤ Apply Filter/Sort from the main menu.

6. To remove the filter, click on the Show all Records button in the tool bar (the third button after Filter/Sort) or select Records ➤ Show All Records from the main menu. You can reapply the filter by repeating step 4.

See Also *Queries*; see *Expressions* for valid filter expressions and examples.

To Remove a Filter

To remove the filter and view all records, click on the Remove Filter button (the third button in the Filter/Sort button set), or select Records ➤ Show All Records from the main menu.

To Save a Filter as a Query

Once your filter works as you desire, you can convert the filter into a query for subsequent execution. Open the Filter Design window by clicking on the Edit Filter/Sort button or the Filter/Sort button in the tool bar. Select File ➤ Save As Query from the main menu, and enter the name of the query.

To Use Existing Queries as Filters

If you want to apply a query for the same table or query as the form or query you are working with, and the query is not an action query or a crosstab query, *and* the query does not include totals, you can use the query as a filter. This method allows you to apply temporarily the criteria specified in a query. A filter looks at the records in the current dynaset, while a query creates a new dynaset.

1. Display the Filter window.

2. Select File ➤ Load from Query.

3. Select the query from the list and select OK.

4. Click on the Apply Filter/Sort button in the tool bar, or select Records ➤ Apply Filter/Sort from the main menu.

See Also   *Queries*

FINDING DATA

To find a specific record or specific value in a single field or all fields of a table or dynaset, use Access' find feature.

To Find a Value in a Record

1. Display your table in Form or Datasheet view. (If you are in Design view, switch to Form view or Datasheet view.)

2. Select the column or field you want to search, if you are searching for a value in a single field.

3. Click on the Find button in the tool bar (it looks like a pair of binoculars; the tool bar is illustrated on the inside front cover), press F7, or select Edit ➤ Find from the main menu.

4. In the Find What box, type the string you want to find. You can use wildcards in this search string. See *Expressions, The Like Operator* for more information on wildcards.

5. In the Where box, select where you want to look for the value. Select Start of Field (the field must begin with the search string), Any Part of Field (the string can appear anywhere within the field), or Match Whole Field (the string must match the entire contents of a field).

6.   In the Search In box, select whether you want Access to search the currently selected field (this is the fastest option, especially if the field is an index) or all fields in a table or dynaset.

7.   Select the direction to search: Up searches from the current record to the beginning of the database; Down searches from the current record to the end of the database.

8.   If you want the search to match upper-and lowercase letters, check the Match Case box.

9.   If you want to search for data in exactly the same format as the search string, check the Search Fields as Formatted box. This option searches data as it is formatted in the table.

10.   To find the first occurrence of the search string, check the Find First button. To find the next occurrence of the search string, check the Find Next button.

To Find and *Replace* a Value

To find a text value within a database and replace it with another:

1.   Display the form or datasheet in Form or Datasheet view. (If you are in Design view, switch to Form view or Datasheet view.)

2.   Select the column or field you want to search, if you are searching for a value in a single field.

3.   Select Edit ➤ Replace from the main menu.

4.   In the Find What box, type the string you want to find. You can use wildcards in this search string. See *Expressions, The Like Operator* for more information on wildcards.

5.   Enter the replacement string in the Replace With box.

6.   In the Search In box, select whether you want Access to search the selected field (this is the fastest option, especially if the field is an index) or all fields in a table or dynaset.

7.   If you want the search to match upper- and lowercase letters, check the Match Case box.

8.   If you want to completely replace the Find What text string with the Replace With text string, check the Match Whole Field box.

9.   Select Find Next (to find but not replace the value), Replace (to find and replace the next occurrence), or Replace All (to replace all values in the table or dynaset).

● **TIP**   To find a value quickly, start Find mode by pressing F7. To find and replace a value, press Shift-F7.

FONTS

Access supports TrueType and PostScript fonts. Fonts add variety to text in forms, reports, and datasheets.

To Change the Font of Text in a Form or Report

To change the font used to display text in a form or report:

1.   Open the form or report in Design view. See *Design View* for more information.

2.   Select the text you want to change.

3.   Click on the font box in the tool bar, and select the font name.

4.   Click on the font size box and select the font size.

5.   Select the special effects you want (bold, italic, or underline).

See Also   *Properties*

To Change the Font
of Text in a Datasheet View

To select a different font for all text displayed in a Datasheet view:

1. Open a datasheet.

2. Select Layout ➤ Font from the main menu.

3. Select the font, style, and size, and check any effects that you want. A sample of your selection is displayed in the window.

4. Select OK.

5. The text in all columns of the datasheet is changed to the selected font. Access also adjusts row height as appropriate to accommodate larger fonts.

FORMS

Forms are screens that can display information and let you edit data in a layout you specify. Forms can consist of a single screen or part of a screen, or can span several screens. To simplify your work, you can create forms that look like your current data-entry form.

To Create a Form

To create a new form:

1. From the Database window, select the Form button.

2. Select New.

3. Access asks you for the name of the table or query to use for the form. Type the name of the table or query, or click on the down-pointing arrow to display the list of available tables and queries, and select one.

4. Click on the Blank Form button to set up the form yourself. Click on the FormWizards button to have Access lead you through the basic form design steps.

See Also *Reports; Macros; Queries; Layering Access Objects*

FORMS AND FORMWIZARDS

FormWizards simplify the creation of a form from scratch. FormWizards allow you to create columnar reports (with fields displayed vertically, one record per page), tabular reports (with fields displayed horizontally, so many records can be displayed on a page), graphs, and form/subform combinations. They also set the fonts, create headers with the current date and footers with the page number, and can add 3D effects for text boxes and labels.

Forms created by a FormWizard can be modified or used as they are.

To Create a Form with FormWizards

1. Move to the Database window by pressing F11.

2. Select the Form button.

3. Select the New button. Access displays the New Form dialog box, shown in Figure III.10.

4. Click the down-pointing arrow key and select the table that contains the fields you want to include on the form.

5. Select the FormWizards button. The FormWizard asks a series of questions.

6. The FormWizard first asks what style of form you want. A single-column form lists one record per screen, with fields placed vertically, one above another. A tabular form looks like a spreadsheet: fields are laid out horizontally. Select the form style you waant and select OK.

7. The FormWizard asks which fields you want to include on the form. Highlight the field you want at the beginning of the form and click on the > button. The field name is

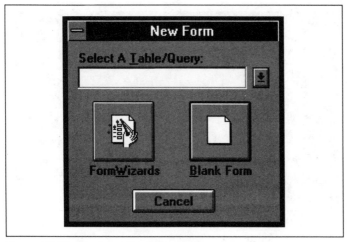

Figure III.10: The New Form dialog box.

removed from the *Available fields* list and added to the *Field order on form* list. In a similar fashion include all the fields you want on the form. Select the Next> button.

8. Select the look of the form. When you select a format, the FormWizard displays a sample in the magnifying glass at the left of the FormWizard window. The FormWizard for this step is displayed in Figure III.11. Select the Next> button.

9. The FormWizard asks for the form name. This name will appear in the Database window list when you select Forms. Enter the name and select the Open button. The FormWizard launches the form and fills the form with the first record in the table.

In addition to the fields you selected, the FormWizard includes a report title and a horizontal line separating the title from the data. It also fills in a background color on the form.

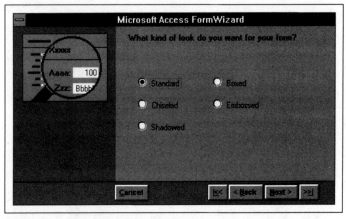

Figure III.11: The FormWizard asks for the kind of look you want for the report.

To Save a Form

To save a form for future use:

1. If the form is in Design view, select File ➤ Save and skip to step 3.

2. If the form is in Form view, select File ➤ Save Form.

3. If this is the first time you have saved the form, Access asks you to name the form. Enter the form name in Form Name box and select OK.

To Save a Form Using a Different Name

To keep a copy of a modified form separate from the original form you edited, select File ➤ Save As (in Design view) or File ➤ Save Form As (in Datasheet or Form view). Enter the new form name and select OK.

To Copy an Existing Form

To copy an existing form to another file:

1. In the Database window, highlight the form and open it in Design view. See *Design View* for more information.

2. Select File ➤ Save As and enter the new form name.

To Delete an Existing Form

To delete an existing form from a database:

1. In the Database window, highlight the form you want to delete.

2. Press Del. Access asks you to confirm your request. You can also delete the form by selecting Edit ➤ Cut, but Access does not ask you to confirm your request with this technique.

3. To undelete a form deleted by mistake, select Edit ➤ Undo Cut from the main menu. You can only undelete the most recently deleted object.

USING FORM HEADERS AND FOOTERS

Headers in forms can be used to display a title and the current date and/or time. Page headers and footers and form headers and footers are called *sections*.

Footers in forms can be used to display page numbers or other information, such as a report date or name, in a smaller font.

To Add a Header to a Form

To add a header or footer section to a form:

1. Open the form in Design view. See *Design View* for more information.

2. Select Layout ➤ Form Hdr/Ftr to add a header to the top (or a footer to the bottom) of the form. Select Layout ➤ Page Hdr/Ftr to add a header to the top (or a footer to the bottom) of a printed page (but not the form itself).

3. Select Header or Footer.

4. Add the text (labels) and/or controls you want. For example, to add a current date, add an unbound text box, and enter the value **DATE()** in the box. When you move to Form view (or print the form), Access displays (or prints) the system date.

Figure A.12 in the Appendix shows a report design in Design view that contains report sections.

CHANGING THE SIZE OF A FORM OR FORM SECTION

The default size of a form or form section may not suit your purpose. Here is how to change the size of a form or form sections.

To Change the Height of a Form Section

To increase or decrease the height of a section of a form:

1. Open the form in Design view. See *Design View* for more information.

2. To change the height of a section, move the pointer to the top or bottom border of the section. The cursor turns into an up-and-down solid arrow with a solid line through it.

3. Click and drag up or down until the section is the size you want.

Similarly, change the width by moving the mouse to the left or right border and dragging the double-headed arrow so the section is the size you desire.

To Change the Size of the Form Display

You can change the size of the Form view automatically so that Access only displays complete records (or as much of a single record as possible).

With the form in Form view, select Window ➤ Size to Fit Form from the main menu.

The behavior of Size to Fit Form is dependent on the Default View property of the form. When the Default View is set to Continuous Forms, if the window shows more than one record at a time, the last record appears either in its entirety or not at all. If the form only displays one record, the window expands to show as much of the record as possible.

When the Default View property is set to Single Form, Access shrinks the window if a record does not occupy the entire screen, and expands the window to show as much of a record as possible when the entire record cannot be displayed at once.

To Attach a Menu to a Form

You can add a custom menu bar to any form. This gives your end user control over specific functions and allows you to execute macros when the user selects a menu option.

1. Create a macro group for each menu.

2. Create the menu bar macro.

- The Action column should contain the Add Menu action.

- The Menu Name for each argument should be set to the text that appears on the menu itself.

- The Menu Macro Name should be set to the name of the macro group that contains the macro that will be run when the menu item is selected.

- The Status Bar Text property contains the text to appear at the bottom of the screen (in the status bar) when the menu item is selected (clicked).

3. When you've added all the menu items, save the macro.

4.   Open in Design mode the form that uses this menu.

5.   Set the form's On Menu property to the name of the macro (the name you gave the macro in step 3).

6.   The menu appears when you view the form in Form view.

See Also   *Macros; Controls; Properties*

To Set Form Properties

Like controls on a form, a form can have its own set of properties. To set or change the properties:

1.   Open the form in Design view. See *Design View* for more information.

2.   Click anywhere in the form not occupied by a control, or select Edit ➤ Select Form from the main menu.

3.   Select View ➤ Properties from the main menu.

4.   Edit the form properties, then click outside the Form Property window to save your changes.

To Use a Different Table or Query for a Form

If you have designed a form and want to use a different table or query for the form:

1.   Open the form in Design view. See *Design View* for more information.

2.   Use Edit ➤ Select Form to select the form.

3.   Open the Properties window by selecting the Properties button (illustrated on the inside front cover) or selecting View ➤ Properties from the main menu.

4.   In the cell to the right of the Record Source property, enter the new table or query you want to use. (Alternatively, select the table or query from the list.)

SUBFORMS

Subforms are forms that are included in other forms. They are generally used to represent the "many" side of a one-to-many relationship.

A subform is simply a form that is smaller than full-screen. As with any form, a subform is attached to a table or set of tables. A form inserted into another form is called a subform, but technically remains a separate, modifiable entity.

To Insert a Subform in a Form

To place a subform in a form:

1. Display the form that will include the subform in Design view. This is called the main form. See *Design View* for more information about displaying a form in Design view.

2. Display the Database Window by pressing F11.

3. Click on the Form button and highlight the name of the form to be used as the subform.

4. Drag the subform on to the main form.

When a subform is included on a form, you can edit it directly. With the main form in Design view, double-click the subform and Access displays a separate editing window for the form. Save the changes (select File ➤ Save from the main menu) and close the subform, and the changes to the subform are reflected in the main form.

PRINTING A FORM

Access allows you to print your data using the layout of your form.

To Preview a Form

To see how the form displayed on your screen will look when printed, open the form in Design view, Form view, or Datasheet view. Click on the Print Preview button on the tool bar (it looks like a piece of paper with a magnifying glass over it), or select File ➤ Print Preview.

You can also preview a form from the Database window. Select the Form button, highlighting the form name, and select File ➤ Print Preview. Access displays a sample of the printout, as shown in Figure A.11 in the Appendix.

From within Print Preview you can select any of these buttons:

Print	Prints the form as it is displayed. Access asks you for the print settings, such as which pages to print.
Setup	Sets the default printer, page size, orientation, and margins.
Zoom	Enlarges the print preview area
Cancel	Returns you to the form or datasheet

See Also *Printing*

To Print a Form

To create a printout of a form:

1. Select File ➤ Print Setup and set the default printer, page size, orientation, and margins.

2. Select File ➤ Print from the main menu.

3. Set the print options (for example, which pages to print), and select OK.

To Make a Form Read-Only

To allow your users to view data but not change it, set the form to read-only.

1. Open the form in Design view. See *Design View* for more information.

2. Click anywhere inside the form window not occupied by a control, or select Edit ➤ Select From from the main menu.

3. Select View ➤ Properties from the main menu.

4. Set the Default Editing property to Read Only. Set the Allow Editing property to Unavailable. Click outside of the Form Property window to save your choices.

MANAGING DATA WITH FORMS

You can edit data by modifying records in Form view or Datasheet view.

To Modify Data in a Form

To change values in a record displayed in Form view:

1. To change a field's contents, click on the field with the mouse, or press Tab until the text in the field to be modified is displayed in reverse video. You can also move to a field by selecting it from the Field drop-down list box on the tool bar.

2. To replace the contents of a field, be sure the text is displayed in reverse video. If it is not, press F2. As you type the first character of the new value, the original value disappears.

3. If you change your mind or make a mistake and do *not* want to update the field, press Esc or click on the Undo button in the tool bar (the second button from the right). To accept the new value, press Enter, Tab, Shift-Tab or other navigation key, or click on another field.

4. If you have made an error within the record and want to return to the original value for *all fields* in the record, select Edit ➤ Undo Current Record from the main menu. You must select this option *before* moving to another record.

See Also   *Editing Data*

To Enter a New Record

There are two ways to add a record. Here's Option 1:

1. Select Records ➤ Go To ➤ New from the main menu.

2. Enter the data in the appropriate fields. Use Tab to move to the next field and Shift-Tab to move to the previous field. Pressing Tab after the last field on a form moves you to another record.

3. To add another record, press the Page Down key, or press Tab when you are in the last field.

4. To return to viewing all records, select Records ➤ Go To ➤ First.

Here's Option 2:

1. Select Records ➤ Data Entry from the main menu or press Ctrl-+.

2. Enter the data in the appropriate fields. Use Tab to move to the next field. Use Shift-Tab to move to the previous field. Pressing Tab after the last field on a form moves you to another record.

3. To add another record, press the Page Down key, or press Tab when you are in the last field.

4. To return to viewing all records, select Records ➤ Show All Records.

To Delete a Record

If the table from which you want to delete records is not related to another table, you can delete records easily. If the table *is* related to another table (as in a one-to-many relationship), you must delete all records from the "many" side of the relationship before deleting records from the "one" side.

1. Display the record that you want to delete. You can use the Find feature to find it, write a query to include the record in a dynaset, use the Page Up or Page Down keys to locate it, or select the record number and enter the number in the Record box at the bottom of the screen. You can also use the menus: Select Records ➤ Go To, then the record you want (for example First, Last, etc.).

2. Select Edit ➤ Select Record from the main menu.

3. You can delete the record in one of four ways:

- select Edit ➤ Cut;
- select Edit ➤ Delete;
- press Ctrl-X; or
- press the Delete key.

4. Access asks you to confirm your delete request. Select Yes to delete the record, or Cancel to keep the record.

Moving around a Form

You can move between records using the VCR-buttons on the bottom of the form. To view a specific record, enter its record number to the right of Record: in the VCR-button area and press Enter.

If a form is longer than one page, you can press Page Down to move down one screen. When Access reaches the end of the form (or if the form is only one screen in length), press Page Down to move to the next record.

To move up when viewing a multi-screen form, press Page Up. When Access reaches the top of the form (or if the form is only one screen in length), press the Page Up key to move to the previous record.

FORMATS

Formats control the display of a field. For example, a date format specifies whether the date is displayed as *01/02/95* or *02 JAN 95*.

You can set the format of a field using the Format Property. There are predefined formats for dates and numbers (including currency). The standard format properties include default values for the DecimalPlaces property (DecimalPlaces is set to Auto). You can override the number of digits to the right of the decimal point by entering a value in the DecimalPlaces property.

Standard Number and Currency Formats

Currency	Uses thousands separator, sets DecimalPlaces property to 2 by default, and displays negative numbers between parentheses in red
Fixed	Displays at least one decimal (so zero always shows as 0); DecimalPlaces property is set to 2 by default
General	Displays value as entered
Percent	Displays value as a percent after multiplying value by 100, then appends the percent sign (%), and sets DecimalPlaces property to 2 by default
Scientific	Uses scientific notation (for example, 1.23E100)
Standard	Uses thousands separator, sets Decimal Places property to 2

Standard Date Formats

Select one of the following formats for the Format Property of a Date and Time field. July 4, 1994, 1:23 p.m. appears as follows:

Format Name	Displayed as
General date	7/4/94; 01:23PM
Short Date	7/4/94
Medium Date	04-Jul-94
Long Date	Varies according to setting in Windows' Control Panel. For example: Monday, July 4, 1994
Short Time	13:23
Medium Time	01:23 PM
Long Time	1:23:00 PM

See Also   *Dates*

Custom Numeric and Currency Formats

You can create your own format string using the characters shown below. A format string can specify four formats:

- the format when the number is positive;
- the format when the number is negative;
- the format when the number is zero; and
- the format when the number is null.

For example, a format string for a numeric field called Price might look like this:

#,##0;(#,##0);"Free";"Price Not Set"

If the value is positive, it will be shown with commas as necessary. If the value is negative, it will be displayed in parentheses and with commas as needed. If the value is 0, Access displays the text string *Free*. If the value is null (that is, a value has not been entered for the field), Access displays the text string *Price Not Set*.

The following characters are used in custom numeric formats:

Character	Purpose
.	decimal separator (actual character used is set in Windows control panel)
,	Thousands separator
0	Placeholder for a digit; 0 if no digit in this position
#	Placeholder for a digit; space if no digit in this position
$	Displays the dollar sign
%	Percent; multiplies value by 100 and appends the percent sign (%)

Character	Purpose
E- or e-	Scientific notation with minus sign next to E or e if negative exponent. Used in conjunction with other symbols
E+ or e+	Scientific notation with minus sign next to E or e if negative exponent, and plus sign (+) next to E or e if positive exponent

Custom Date and Time Formats

You can create your own format string using these characters:

:	separates hours from minutes, minutes from seconds. The actual separator character is defined in the Windows control panel.
/	separates month, day, and year
AM/PM	12-hour clock, AM or PM in uppercase
am/pm	12-hour clock, am or pm in lowercase
A/P	12-hour clock, A or P in uppercase
a/p	12-hour clock, a or p in lowercase
AMPM	12-hour clock, morning/afternoon text defined in Windows control panel
d	day of month (one digit for 1–9, two digits for 10–31)
dd	day of month (01–09, then 10–31)
ddd	day of weekday (three letters: Mon, Tue, Wed. …)
dddd	day of week spelled out (Monday, Tuesday, Wednesday …)
ddddd	month/day/year (same as Short Date format); displays according to the international settings in Windows.

dddddd	Weekday, Month dd, year (same as Long Date format); displays according to the international settings in Windows.
h	hour (one digit if 0–9, two digits if 10–23)
hh	hour (two digits, 01–23)
m	month (one digit if 1–9, two digits if 10–12)
mm	month (two digits, 01–12)
mmm	month abbreviation (Jan, Feb, Mar…)
mmmm	month spelled out (January, February, March…)
n	minute (one digit if 0–9, two digits if 10–59)
nn	minute (two digits, 00–59)
q	quarter of the year in which date occurs (1 through 4)
s	second (one digit if 0–9, two digits if 10–59)
ss	seconds (two digits, 00–59)
ttttt	long time format (for example, 11:02:03 AM)
w	day of week (1–7; 1 is Sunday)
ww	week of the year (1–52)
y	day number (1–366)
yy	year (two digits, 00–99)
yyyy	year (four digits, 0100–9999)

See Also   *Properties*

FOXPRO

Data stored in a FoxPro formatted file can be used in Access. Similarly, data stored in Access can be saved in FoxPro format for use by other applications.

To Save Tables in FoxPro Format

To create a copy of an Access table in FoxPro format:

1. Close the table. If you are working in a multiuser environment, all users must close the table.

2. Open the Database window by pressing F11.

3. Select File ➤ Export from the main menu. Access displays the Export dialog box.

4. In the Data Destination text box, select the FoxPro format, then select OK.

5. From the list of tables in the current database, select the table you want to export, then select OK.

6. Enter the name of the file you want to export *to*.

7. Access adjusts field names if they are too long or do not conform to FoxPro standards (for example, if they contain spaces).

To Use FoxPro Files

To attach or import a file from a FoxPro database:

1. Be sure a Microsoft Access database is open.

2. Select File ➤ Attach Table from the main menu to attach a FoxPro file. Select File ➤ Import to import a FoxPro file.

3. Select FoxPro as the Data Source.

4. Select the FoxPro file you want to use. FoxPro files have the .DBF extension.

5. If you *import* the file, Microsoft Access creates the table automatically, and your task is complete. Repeat step 4 until you have selected all needed files. Click on Close.

6. If you *attach* the file, Microsoft Access prompts you for the FoxPro index file name(s). Index files have the file extension .NDX for single indexes and .MDX for files containing multiple indexes. Select each index file you need. Click on Close when you are done.

See Also   *Attach a Database File; Import a Database File; Export a Table*

GRAPHICS

You can use graphics to add variety to a form or report, or to add images such as logos to other business documents (data-entry forms, employment applications, and so on).

ADDING A GRAPHIC
IMAGE TO A FORM OR REPORT

You can easily add or modify graphic images on a form or report. You can add a bound field to a form or report to display a picture whose contents are stored in a field in a table; the field must have a data type of OLE Object. Unbound fields display the same image on each form or page of a report, which is useful for displaying company logos.

To Resize a Graphic Object

1. Click on the object's control.

2. When the black dots surround the control, point at any one of them. When the pointer changes to a two-headed arrow, drag the dot to resize the object.

To Resize a Graphic Object's Frame

To expand or contract the object frame to exactly match the image it contains:

1. Click on the control.

2. Move the pointer over any of the black boxes that surround the image so that the pointer changes to a two-headed arrow, then double-click.

To Adjust the Proportion of a Graphic Object

If a picture's dimensions do not match the dimensions of the control on the form or report, you can adjust the object's scale in several ways.

1. Open the form or report in Design view. See *Design View* for more information.

2. Select the graphic object.

3. Click on the Properties button in the tool bar, or select View ➤ Properties from the main menu.

4. In the Scaling property, enter one of these values:

- Select *Clip* to display the graphic without any changes to the scale. If the picture does not completely fit, Access displays as much of the image as it can. Clip is the default property.

- Select *Scale* to change the dimension of the object to fit within the frame; Access changes the aspect ratio (proportions) to accommodate the graphic.

- Select *Zoom* to keep the same aspect ratio (proportions) but display the entire image. This may result in white space on one side of the image.

GRAPHS

With graphs, you can quickly display numeric data in a form that emphasizes proportions, trends, and relationships. Access includes Microsoft Graph to handle the graphing and charting tasks.

To Create a Graph with Data in Access

A graph can be based on information in an Access table or query, or on data outside Access (for example, data in a spreadsheet). The following directions work with data in Access.

1. Open the form or report in Design view. See *Design View* for more information.

2. Click on the Graph button in the toolbox (illustrated on the inside front cover).

3. Move the pointer to the form. Click on the upper-left corner of the control and drag to the bottom-right corner, then release the mouse button.

4. Access displays the GraphWizard, which leads you through the basic steps of creating a chart. The Graph-Wizard asks which table or query to use as a source, and which field should be graphed, as well as the title and type graph.

5. When the GraphWizard is finished, a graph appears on your form.

To Create a Graph Using Data outside Access

You can include a graph using data from another file, including a spreadsheet. To create a chart, add an unbound object frame to the form or report:

1. Open the form or report in Design view. See *Design View* for more information.

2. Click on the unbound object frame in the toolbox. The toolbox is illustrated on the inside front cover.

3. Move the pointer to the form. Click on the upper-left corner of the control and drag to the bottom-right corner, then release the mouse button.

4. Select Microsoft Graph as the object type you want to embed.

5. The Graph application opens. Use Graph to create the chart you want.

6. Within Graph, select File ➤ Exit and Return.

7. Graph asks if you want to update the graph in Microsoft Access. Choose Yes.

To Change Access Graphs

To change the style, type, title, legend, and other characteristics of a chart or graph:

1. Open the form containing the graph in Form view, the report in Report view, or either object in Design view. See *Design View* for more information.

2. Double-click on the graph object.

3. Access launches Microsoft Graph with two windows. The first contains the Datasheet containing the values to be graphed. The other window, titled *Microsoft Access - Chart*, shows the chart as it is currently defined. These windows are shown in Figure A.15 in Appendix.

4. Click anywhere within the chart, then select from these main menu options:

- To change the type of chart, select Gallery from the main menu.
- To change the title, legends, axes, or data labels, select Chart from the main menu.

- To change patterns displayed in the chart (such as the pattern in a pie slice), select Format ➤ Patterns from the main menu.

- You can also double-click on the element you want to change, such as the chart's title.

5. To annotate a chart, select Chart ➤ Add Arrow.

To Change the Chart Type

To change the type of chart:

1. Double-click the graphic object to launch Microsoft Graph.

2. Select Format ➤ Chart from the main menu.

3. If Access displays the Format Chart dialog box, shown in Figure III.12, click on the type of chart you want and select OK to change the graph type. Do not complete the next steps.

- Select Custom to change more chart details; proceed to step 4.

- If you have already selected a chart type, Access displays the Format Chart dialog box. Proceed to step 4.

4. In the Format Chart dialog box, you can select another Chart Type, then click on the variations of that chart type. Some chart formats, such as bar/column charts and pie charts, have special characteristics that can be set in this dialog box. Select OK when you've made your selections.

GRIDS

In Design view, Access provides grids to help you align and resize controls. (See *Forms, To Change the Size of the Form Display*). See *Design View* for more information about viewing and modifying an object's design.

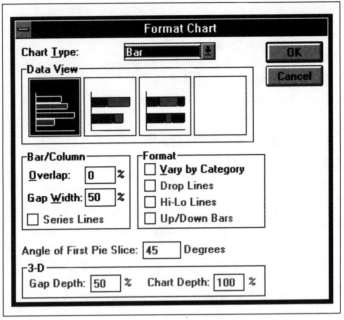

Figure III.12: The Format Chart dialog box

To display a grid for a form or report, select View ➤ Grid from the main menu.

To change the number of points in a grid, open the Property window for the form. Set the GridX and GridY properties to larger numbers to increase the number of gridpoints.

See Also   *Queries; Datasheet; Properties*

GROUPING DATA

To specify subtotals in queries, you can use the Group By field to specify breaks in the sort order. Group By also summarizes records in the field specified as "Group By". For example, a query can return one record summarizing all data for a state by specifying "Group By" in the Total row of a query for the State field.

To Summarize and Group Data by a Field Value

To include a grouping for data and summarize data when the value in the group field changes:

1. Open a query in Design view. See *Design View* for more information.

2. Enter the field name in the Field row, or drag the name from the table windows at the top of the form to the Field row.

3. If the Total line is not displayed in the QBE grid, select View ➤ Totals from the main menu.

4. In the Total line of the field, select Group By.

To Set the Interval of a Group

When you create a group report, you can specify the range of values included in each group as follows:

1. Open the report in Design view.

2. Open the Sorting and Grouping window by selecting View ➤ Sorting and Grouping from the main menu. The window is shown in Figure III.13 with some settings displayed in the grid.

3. Select the field you want to group on. In the Group Properties window, enter the type of group you want in the cell to the right of Group On.

4. In the cell to the right of Group Interval, enter the range of values to be included in a group. For example, if the field has a numeric data type, and the Group On value is set to Each Value, enter 100 in the Group Interval cell. Access will group your records in 100's (0–99, 100–199, and so on).

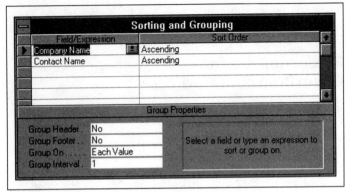

Figure III.13: The Sorting and Grouping window

5.   Close the Sorting and Grouping window by double-clicking in the window's Control menu box.

See Also   *Sort Order*

HEADERS AND FOOTERS

Headers and footers are special sections on a report usually used to hold information such as a report's title, the current date and time, page numbers, and an "End of Report" indicator. In addition, a report footer is often used for report totals or record counts.

REPORT HEADERS AND FOOTERS

A *report header* is printed or displayed only at the beginning of the report. A *report footer* is printed or displayed only at the end of the report.

To Add or Remove a Report Header or Footer

To add or delete a report header or a report footer:

1. Open the report in Design view. See *Design View* for more information.

2. Select Layout ➤ Report Hdr/Ftr to toggle the header or footer band on or off.

Access puts a check mark next to the menu option when the report header and footer are added to the report.

PAGE HEADERS AND FOOTERS

A *page header* appears at the top of every page. Page headers are useful for column headings. A *page footer* appears at the bottom of every page. Page footers are useful for displaying page numbers.

To Add or Remove a Page Header or Footer

To add or delete a page header or footer:

1. Open the report in Design view. See *Design View* for more information.

2. Select Layout ➤ Page Hdr/Ftr to toggle the header or footer band on or off.

Access puts a check mark next to the menu option when the page header and footer is added to the report. Once you select Page Hdr/Ftr, Access changes the Layout menu so it has two entries: Page Hdr/Ftr and Report Hdr/Ftr. Each of these has a check mark if active.

GROUP HEADERS AND FOOTERS

A *group header* is displayed at the beginning of a new group of data (such as when the value of a field changes). A *group footer* is displayed at the end of a group of data, and is used most often to display subtotals (the total of the group).

To Add or Remove a Group Header or Group Footer

To add or remove a group header or footer, you must have at least one group defined for the report.

1. Open the report in Design view. See *Design View* for more information.

2. Select the Sorting and Grouping button on the tool bar (illustrated on the inside back cover), or select View ➤ Sorting and Grouping from the main menu.

3. You must have at least one field defined on the first Sorting and Grouping line. Select a field name or enter an expression in the Field/Expression column. Select a sort order (*ascending* for A–Z order, *descending* for Z–A order) in the Sort Order box.

4. To add a group header to the report, set the Group Header property to Yes. Similarly, to add a group footer, set the Group Footer property to Yes. (No is the default property value for the Group Header and Group Footer properties.)

Group headers can also be used to display *part* of a group value. For example, if an accounting code is made up of 2 four-characters codes, separated by a hyphen (such as *A100-2000*), you can create group breaks every time the first four characters of the code change.

To Print Part of a Group Value in the Group Header

1. Open the report in Design view. See *Design View* for more information.

2. Select the Sorting and Grouping button on the tool bar (illustrated on the inside front cover), or select View ➤ Sorting and Grouping from the main menu.

3. Set the Field/Expression column to the field name or expression that contains the values you want to group the report by. (In the accounting example, the field might be Account Code.)

4. Set the Group Header property to Yes by entering **Yes** in the cell to the right of *Group Header*.

5. Set the Group Footer property to No by entering **No** in the cell to the right of *Group Footer*.

6. Set the Group On property to Prefix Characters by clicking on the down-pointing arrow and selecting the option.

7. Set the Group Interval property to the number of characters to use in the group header value. (In the accounting example above, the property value should be set to **4**.)

8. Select the text box button from the toolbox. (If the toolbox is not displayed, select View ➤ Toolbox from the main menu.) The toolbox is illustrated on the inside front cover.

9. Add a text box to the group header. Select a text box from the toolbox and drag it into the Group Header section.

10. Select the Properties button in the tool bar, or select View ➤ Properties from the main menu.

11. In the cell to the right of *Control Source*, enter an expression to define the characters to be printed. (In the accounting example, you would enter **=Left([Account Code],4)** in the Control Source cell.)

You can use group headers to separate the first character of a group, such as for a heading in an employee telephone directory. The first group header could display *A*, after which all the employees with a last name beginning with *A* would be listed. The next group header could display *B*, followed by all employees with last names beginning with *B*, and so on.

To print part of a group value in the group header (for example, for headings in a telephone directory):

1. Open the report in Design view. See *Design View* for more information.

2. Select the Sorting and Grouping button on the tool bar, or select View ➤ Sorting and Grouping from the main menu.

3. Set the Field/Expression column of the *first* line to the field name or expression that contains the values you want to group the report by. (For example, you might use the Last Name field.)

4. Set the Group Header property to Yes.

5. Set the Group Footer property to No.

6. Set the Group On property to Prefix Characters.

7. Set the Group Interval property to the number of characters to use in the group header value. (In the telephone directory example above, set the property value to **1**.)

8. Set the Field/Expression column of the *second* line to the field name or expression that contains the values you want to sort the report by. Select the same field selected in step 3.

9. Set the Group Header property to No.

10. Set the Group Footer property to No.

11. Set the Group On property to Each Value.

12. Set the Group Interval property to 1.

13. Select the text box button from the toolbox. (If the toolbox is not displayed, select View ➤ Toolbox from the main menu.) The toolbox is illustrated on the inside front cover.

14. Add a text box to the group header.

15. Select the Properties button in the tool bar, or select View ➤ Properties from the main menu.

16. In the Control Source box, enter an expression to define the characters to be printed. (Using the Last Name example, enter **=Left([Last Name],1)** in the Control Source box.)

HELP

Access offers both the traditional Windows help system and step-by-step help.

You can bring up the Windows help system text by pressing F1 at any time. If you are in the middle of a procedure, Access may display context-sensitive help based on the task it thinks you are trying to accomplish.

To get step-by-step help, you can view Cue Cards. Cue Cards describe the individual steps needed to accomplish a task. Cue Cards remain visible on your screen while you work with Access, so you can see the instructions *and* your own work at the same time.

You can also press Shift-F1. The pointer changes to a question mark, which you click on the item you want help about.

To Get Help

To open the help system's main screen:

1. Click on the Help button in the tool bar. The Help button is the last button on the right of the tool bar, and has a question mark on its face. Alternatively, select Help ➤ Contents from the main menu or press F1.

2. Select the top of interest, or click on the Cue Cards window to display a list of available Cue Card subjects.

To Get Help on a Selected Subject

To open the help system and read about a selected subject:

1. Click on the Help button in the tool bar. The Help button is the last button on the right of the tool bar, and has a question mark on its face. Alternatively, select Help ➤ Contents from the main menu or press F1.

   • Help ➤ Contents takes you to a different place in the help system than the Help button or F1.

2. Click on the Search button and enter the topic, or select the topic name from the list box.

● **TIP**   You can go directly to the Search dialog box by selecting Help ➤ Search from the main menu.

To Use Cue Cards

To view the Cue Cards for a task, select Help ➤ Cue Cards from the main menu. Access displays a menu of available Cue Cards. Click on the > button to the left of the subject you want to read. Alternatively, open the help system and select the Cue Cards subject.

Figure III.14 displays a sample Cue Card.

IMPORT A DATABASE FILE

When you import a data from another format (Btrieve, dBASE, Fox-Pro, or Paradox, for example), you copy it to an Access table and save it in Access's own format. You work with a *copy* of the file in Access, *not* the original file.

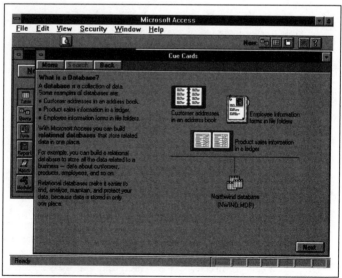

Figure III.14: A Cue Card

Importing data is different from attaching data. When you attach a database from another format, Access reads and writes data using the original database. No copy is made, and the original database is not converted to Access's own format.

See Also   *Attach a Database File*

To Import a Database

To use the data stored in another database:

1. Open the Database window by pressing F11.

2. Select File ➤ Import from the main menu.

3. In the Import dialog box, select the database format of the file you want to import, then select OK.

4. Select the file from the Select File dialog box, then select Import.

See Also   Instructions vary beyond this point depending on the type of database file you are importing. Entries under *Btrieve, dBASE, FoxPro, SQL Databases* or *Paradox* provide specific directions for importing data in these formats. You can also import files in delimited and fixed-length formats. See *Text Files*.

INDEX

When designing a table, you can set an index by selecting a field and assigning the Indexed Property. Memo, yes/no, and OLE object fields cannot be used as indexes.

Indexes are created or removed when you save the table's design. New indexes can be added to existing tables, and existing indexes can be removed in the Table Design window.

Indexes are automatically updated when records are added, changed, or deleted.

The Indexed property for a table's primary key is set to Yes (No Duplicates) by default if the key is a single field. See *Primary Key* for more information.

To Create a Single-Field Index

To create an index on a single field:

1.   Open a table in Design view. See *Design View* for more information.

2.   Select the field to index.

3.   Press F6 to move to the Field Properties window. Press ↓ until you are in the cell following *Indexed*. Alternatively, click in the Indexed property cell.

4.   Enter one of the following in the cell:

- **No**—no index is used

- **Yes (Duplicates OK)**—index is used; two records can contain the same value in this field

- **Yes (No Duplicates)**—index is used; no two records can contain the same value in this field

To Delete a Single-Field Index

To remove an index created from a single field:

1.   Open a table in Design view. See *Design View* for more information.

2.   Select the field to un-index.

3.   Press F6 to move to the Field Properties window. Press ↓ until you are in the cell following *Indexed*. Alternatively, click in the Indexed property cell.

4.   Enter **No** in the property cell.

To Create a Multi-Field Index

You can index a table on more than one field (city, state, and zip code, for example). Up to five multi-field indexes can be defined for a table.

To create a multi-field index:

1. Open a table in Design view. See *Design View* for more information.

2. Click on the Properties button in the tool bar to display the property sheet for the table.

3. Press Tab or ↓ to move to one of the five index property cells, or click directly in the cell. The indexes are labeled Index1 through Index5.

4. Type the field names to be concatenated into the index, separating each field with a semicolon (;). For example, type **city; state; zip** to create a multi-field index that combines the values in the city, state, and zip fields into a single index value.

5. The index will be created when you save the table design or move to Datasheet view.

● **TIP**   You must enter at least two field names in any of the Index1 through Index5 cells. If you enter a single field name, Access will warn you that you must create a single-field index instead.

To Delete a Multi-Field Index

To remove an index created from more than one field:

1. Open a table in Design view. See *Design View* for more information.

2. Click on the Properties button in the tool bar (illustrated on the inside back cover) to display the property sheet for the table.

3.   Press Tab or ↓ to move to one of the index property cells of the index you want to delete, then press Del. Alternatively, click directly in the index property cell, highlight the entry, and press Del.

See Also   *Primary Key*

JOINING TABLES

To use more than one table in a query, you can *join* two or more tables.

Joins permit you to establish one-to-one, one-to-many, and many-to-many relationships between tables.

- In a one-to-one relationship, a record in Table A has no more than one matching record in Table B. For example, suppose you join an Employee table and a Spouse table. An employee record in the Employee table can have no more than one record in the Spouse table (and in fact may have no matching record in the Spouse table).

- In a one-to-many relationship, a record in Table A has zero or more related records in Table B. For example, a record in the Employee table may have many (or no) matching records in a Dependents table.

- In a many-to-many relationship, a record in Table A has zero or more matching records in Table B, and a record in Table B can be related to more than one record in Table A. For example, if a husband and wife who have a child both work for the same company, each will have matching records to a record in the Child table. The child's record will have two relationships back to the Employee table (one for the father, one for the mother).

When you join two or more tables, Access follows the relationship between the tables in order to report all the relationships. For example, suppose your Employee table (which contains an Employee

ID and the employee's name) is related to a Benefits table, and an employee can enroll in a health plan, a life insurance plan, and a retirement plan.

You can join the employee record to an Employee ID field in the Benefits table. When you query the database, Access first looks at the primary table, finds the unique value, then tries to find the same value in the matching field of the related table. When you define a query, you can specify the employee's name from the Employee table and select fields from the Benefits table.

When you run the query, Access can list the employee's name and information about the health plan in the first datasheet row, the employee's name and information about the life insurance plan in the next datasheet row, and the employee's name and information about the retirement plan in the third datasheet row. Because you have a join, Access knows how to find the related information.

When you join two or more tables, you specify the common field between the two tables. The field must have the same data type in both tables.

A table can be related to a primary table and be the primary table in another join. For example, you can join an Employee table to the Benefits table by using an Employee ID number in both tables. The Benefits table can be related to the table that contains the terms and conditions of the benefits stored in the Description table if both tables contain a Benefits Plan Code. Thus the Benefits table is both a primary table (to the Description table) and a related table (to the Employee table).

TYPES OF JOINS

There are three types of joins between a primary table and a related table:

equi-join	Access looks at the primary table, finds the equivalent value in the related table, and reports only those records in the primary table that have matching records in the related table

outer joins	Access reports on all records in the primary table, whether or not they have matching records in the related table. In addition, Access can display all records in the related table that do not have matching records in the primary table, a condition that should not exist if referential integrity has been turned on.
self-join	Access looks up a field value in the key value of the *same* table.

To Join Two or More Tables

You can join tables in one of two ways.

- Define the join for use throughout all objects in the database. When you use the two tables, their relationship is automatically shown in a query.

- Define the join on an ad-hoc basis. When you use the two tables you must explicitly define the connection, which is valid only for the current query.

To Create a Universal Join

To create a join between two tables that is known throughout Access:

1. Open the Database window by pressing F11.

2. Select Edit ➤ Relationships.

3. Access displays the Relationships window, shown in Figure III.15. Select the name of the primary table from the Primary Table drop-down list. The primary table is the one containing the "one" side in a one-to-one or one-to-many relationship. Access automatically fills in the key field from the table under the Primary Key Fields heading.

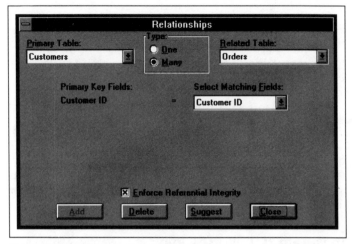

Figure III.15: The Relationships dialog box

4. Select the type of relationship in the Type box.

- If you select One, a record in the primary table can be related to only one record in the related table.

- If you select Many, one record in the primary table can be related to one or more records in the related table.

5. Select the related table from the Related Table pull-down list. This table will be connected to the Primary Table.

6. If Access can find a field in the Related Table that matches the primary key field name from the primary table, it displays the field in the Select Matching Fields pull-down list. Typically, Access displays the field name of the related table's primary key. Alternately, you can ask Access to look for fields with the same name by pressing the Suggest button. If Access' choice is incorrect, click on the down-pointing arrow in the box or press Alt-↓ and select the correct field name.

7. At the bottom of the Relationships window is an Enforce Referential Integrity check box. *Referential integrity* controls how you delete records. With referential integrity on, you cannot delete a record in the primary table if a related record in the related table exists. To enable referential integrity, click on the Enforce Referential Integrity box so that an *X* appears in the box.

8. Select Add, then Close. Access displays the Database window.

● **TIP**   If you specify a related table using an index that permits no duplicates, Access creates a one-to-one relationship no matter what you specify in the Type options box.

To Delete a Universal Join

To remove a join known throughout Access:

1. Open the Database window by pressing F11.

2. Select Edit ➤ Relationships.

3. Access displays the Relationships window. Select the name of the primary table from the Primary Table drop-down list.

4. Select the type of relationship by selecting an option in the Type box.

   • If you select One, a record in the primary table can be related to only one record in the related table.

   • If you select Many, one record in the primary table can be related to one or more records in the related table.

5. Select the related table from the Related Table pull-down list.

6. If Access can find a field in the Related Table that matches the primary key field name from the primary table, it displays the field in the Select Matching Fields pull-down list. Typically, Access displays the field name of the related

table's primary key. If Access' choice is incorrect, click on the down-pointing arrow in the box or press Alt-↓ and select the correct field name.

7.   Select Delete. Access removes the join and displays the Database window.

● **TIP**   When you create a universal join and open the related tables in a query's Design view, a line indicating the relationship is displayed between the related fields.

To Create an Ad-Hoc Inner Join within a Query

Using this method, you can join two or more tables while designing a query. These instructions assume that you are working with an existing query in which all necessary tables have been added (though not joined). To add all tables to a query, specify each table when you create a new query, or select Query ➤ Add Table from the main menu in a query's Design view.

1.   Open a query in Design view. See *Design View* for further information.

2.   Select the field in the primary table you want to related to a field in the related table. Select the field by clicking on it or highlighting it using ↑ or ↓.

3.   Ensure that the field in the related table is displayed in the related table's window. If it is not, use the scroll bars or ↑ and ↓ until the field name appears.

4.   Click and drag the field name from the primary table to the corresponding field name in the related table. The pointer becomes a "no" symbol (a zero with a slash across it). As you move the mouse, the pointer changes into a rectangular box. Drop the box on the field name in the related table.

5.   Access displays a line between the two fields. If the field name moves out of the window, Access displays a line to the window's title bar. Two joined tables are shown in Figure A.16 in Appendix.

To Delete a Join in a Query

To remove a join between two tables in a query:

1. Open the form in Design view. See *Design View* for further information.

2. Click on the line joining the two tables (the join line becomes bold when you click in the right place) and press Del. Access removes the line between the tables.

3. If the join was created in the query, the join is deleted. If the tables are related in a universal join, Access disables (removes) the join for the current query only, but does not remove the universal join itself.

OUTER JOINS

In an outer join, Access queries display all records in the primary table whether or not they have related records in the related table.

There are two types of outer joins:

In a *left outer join*, all records in the primary table are included in the query, along with all records from the related table that have matching values.

In a *right outer join*, all records in the related table are included in the query, along with all records from the primary table that have matching records.

If you select a right outer join, you can look for all records that do not have a matching record in the primary table. This denotes a break in the referential integrity if that feature has been enabled.

To Create an Outer Join

To create an outer join between two tables:

1. Create an inner join. See *To Create an Ad-Hoc Inner Join within a Query* above.

2. Double-click on the line connecting the two tables. Access opens the Join Properties dialog box.

3. Select option 2 in the dialog box to create a left outer join. Select option 3 to create a right outer join.

4. Select OK.

SELF-JOINS

Self-joins are useful in applications that use hierarchical information within the table itself. For example, in a parts table in a manufacturing application, suppose each part is a subassembly of another part. If each record contains a part's number, description, and subassembly part number, you can join the table to itself to list the part's name and subassembly part's name on the same line. In such a case, you can tell Access to find the description using the subassembly part number by looking for that number in the same table.

To Create a Self-Join

To create a self-join (a join of a table to itself):

1. Open the query in Design view. See *Design View* for more information.

2. If the query does not display two windows for the table you want self-joined at the top of the query window, select Query ➤ Add Table and add another copy of the table. Access displays the table name followed by _2 in the second field list window.

3. Join the field from the first field list window to the key field name in the second field list window for the table by dragging the field name from the first window to the second. See *To Create an Ad-Hoc Inner Join within a Query* above for details.

To Change Inner and Outer Joins

To modify an inner or outer join:

1. Open the query in Design view. See *Design View* for more information.

2. Double-click on the line connecting the two tables. Access opens the Join Properties dialog box.

3. Select option 1 in the dialog box to change an outer join to an inner join. Select option 2 to change an inner join or a right outer join to a left outer join. Select option 3 to change an inner join or a left outer join to a right outer join.

4. Select OK.

See Also   *One-to-Many Relationship; One-to-One Relationship*

KEYBOARD SHORTCUTS

See Part II for a list of keyboard shortcuts.

To Assign a Macro to a Key

You can create your own keyboard shortcuts by assigning a macro to a key or key combination:

1. Create a new macro or display a macro in Design view. See *Macros* for details. The Macro window is shown in Figure A.13 in the Appendix.

2.   If the Macro Name column is not displayed, select the
Macro Names button on the tool bar (the first button). Access displays the Macro Name column in the grid.

3.   In the Macro Name column, enter the key or key combination you want to use to execute the macro. See the list of
valid key names below.

4.   Enter the action you want to take when the key or key
combination is pressed. To display a list of options, click
on the down-pointing arrow key (or press Alt-↓), highlight
the option and press Enter. If you want to perform more
than one action, enter the next action in the next row of the
grid, leaving the Macro Names column blank.

5.   Save the macro by selecting File ➤ Save from the main
menu with the name Autokeys.

- You can use a different macro name. Be sure to assign it
  to the Key Assignment Macro: Select View ➤ Options ➤
  Keyboard and enter the macro name in the Key Assignment Macro property. The following key names are
  valid:

^A, ^1	Ctrl plus any letter or number
{F1}, {F2}, etc.	Any function key
^{F1}, ^{F2}, etc.	Ctrl plus any function key
+{F1}, +{F2}, etc.	Shift plus any function key
{INSERT}	Insert (Ins) key
^{INSERT}	Ctrl-Ins
+{INSERT}	Shift-Ins
{DELETE}	Delete (Del) key
^{DELETE} or ^{DEL}	Ctrl-Del
+{DELETE} or +{DEL}	Shift-Del

See Also   *Macros*

LABELS

Labels are used either as headings or captions on forms and reports or to describe the contents or purpose of a text box. Labels display descriptive text and are automatically created when you add a bound control to a form or report.

You can also add text to a label that is not attached to a field in the table, as for report or form headings.

To Add a Label to a Form or Report

To add a text label to a form or report:

1. Open the form or report in Design view. See *Design View* for more information.

2. If the toolbox is not displayed, select View ➤ Toolbox from the main menu. The toolbox is illustrated on the inside front cover.

3. Click on the text button (the button with the large A on it).

4. Click in the upper-left corner of the area in which you want to place the label on the form or report. Drag to the bottom-right corner of the label's desired location and release the mouse button.

5. Access displays a flashing vertical bar inside the label. Type the text for the label. Click outside the label when you are finished.

To Attach a Label to a Control

To attach a text label to an existing control:

1. Select the label tool from the toolbox.

2. Move the pointer to the area on the form where you want the label, click, and drag to size the label.

3. Press Enter or click on the label. Access puts black boxes at the corners of the label.

4. Select Edit ➤ Cut from the main menu or press Ctrl-X.

5. Select the control that you want to attach the label to.

6. Select Edit ➤ Paste from the main menu or press Ctrl-V. Access attaches the label below the control you selected in step 2.

To Change the Text in a Label

You can change the text within a label in two ways:

1. Click directly on the label. When the vertical bar (the *I beam*) appears, make the changes you want and click outside the label to save the new text.

2. Display the property window. (Click on the Properties button in the tool bar, or select View ➤ Properties from the main menu.) The Properties window is displayed in Figure III.16. Press Tab ↓ until you have moved to the cell to the right of *Caption*. Enter the new label text. Click anywhere outside the label, or press Tab, Shift-Tab, ↑, or ↓ to move to another cell.

To Delete a Label

Click on the label, then press Del.

To Disconnect a Label from a Field

Select the label or field, then press Del or select File ➤ Delete.

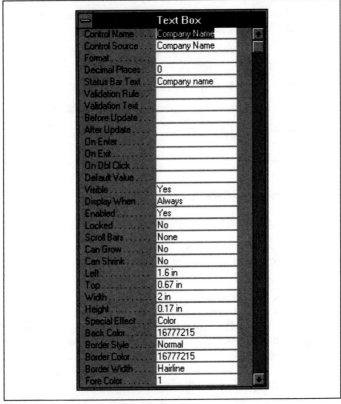

Figure III.16: The Properties window

To Change the Appearance of a Label

Labels are one of the controls Access provides in Design view. Since a label is a control, you can change a label just as you would any other control on a form or report. For example, click on the Palette button or select View ➤ Palette from the main menu to select background and foreground colors and 3D effects. You can also resize or move labels.

See Also   *Controls*

LAYERING ACCESS OBJECTS

Access allows you to build new objects on top of top of existing ones. For example, you can define a query, then build a second query on top of the first query by further refining the criteria. Changes made to the first query are automatically used when you run the second query. Thus, you have layered one query upon another.

Use layered objects when the primary object is complex, and modifying it could cause errors.

Similarly, you can build a report on top of a query, a form on top of a table, and so on, by using the set of buttons marked New in the tool bar.

To Layer Access Objects

To add a new layer to an existing Access object:

1. Move to the base object (a table or query, for example) that will serve as the primary object. You can be in any view, not only Design view.

2. Select the type of object you want to layer on top of the primary object by selecting the New Query, New Form, or New Report button in the tool bar.

3. Access opens a new window (New Query, New Form, or New Report) and automatically fills in the Select a Table/Query box. Proceed to add the new query, form, or report as you would from the Database window.

● **TIP**   Use a parameter query as the primary object in a layered set of objects to create complex processing without using Access Basic Code.

See Also   *Forms; Reports; Macros; Queries*

LINES

You can add lines to forms and reports to draw attention to groups of controls or provide visual breaks on a page.

To Draw a Line on a Form or Report

To add a line to a form or report:

1. Open the form or report in Design view. See *Design View* for more information.

2. If the toolbox is not displayed, select View ➤ Toolbox. The toolbox is shown on the inside front cover.

3. Select the line tool. Click on the form or report at the beginning point of the line, drag to the endpoint, and release the mouse button.

You can modify the control using the same procedures as with any other control. For example, you can delete a line by clicking on it to select it, then pressing Del. You can also move and stretch or shorten lines.

See Also   *Rectangles; Drawing Tools*

LIST BOXES

List boxes resemble combo boxes—both are used to select values. However, you can add a *new* value with a combo box.

See Also   *Combo Boxes*

MACROS

A macro is a set of instructions that allows you to quickly execute instructions within Access. Macros can also be assigned to command buttons, so that clicking a button on a form executes a series of instructions.

A macro group is a set of individual macros that have been entered in a single macro window. Though each macro can be run independently, macro groups typically consist of macros that are related in some way (for example, macros that work on the same table or the same form).

You create and edit macros using the macro's Design view, a window that contains a grid similar to that in Design view for a table or query. Figure A.13 in the Appendix shows this grid with all columns displayed.

To Create a Macro

To create a new macro:

1. Open the Database window by pressing F11.

2. Select the Macro button.

3. Select New. Access opens the Macro Window. The I-beam is in the Action column.

4. Click on the down-pointing arrow at the end of the field in the Action column, or press Alt-↓ to display the action options. Select the action you want.

5. Press Tab to move to the Comments column. Enter a description that explains what action the step takes.

6. The Action Arguments section of the screen displays a set of properties and conditions depending on the action selected in step 4. As you move between the arguments, Access displays explanatory text that suggests what should be entered.

7. To enter another action, move to the next row in the macro grid at the top of the Macro window, and go to step 4.

8. To save the macro, select File ➤ Save from the main menu and enter the name of the macro in the Macro Name box.

● **TIP**   Many action arguments and conditions in a macro (see *To Set Macro Conditions*, below) refer to a control on a form or report. When you need to enter such an argument, enter the argument as **Forms!formname!controlname** or **Reports!reportname!control-name**, where Forms! and Reports! are reserved words and must be used, and an exclamation point must be used between the form or report name and the control name.

To Use Drag-and-Drop to Define Macro Actions

You can add an action to a macro quickly by using drag-and-drop. When you use drag-and-drop, Access sets the action arguments at the bottom of the grid for you automatically.

1. Open the Database window by pressing F11.

2. If you cannot see both the Macro grid and the Database window, select Window ➤ Tile from the main menu.

3. Select the object from the Database window you want to open or run. For example, to have the macro open a table, select the Table button in the Database window. Then select the table you want the macro to open by clicking on it and holding down the mouse button.

4. Drag the table name to the Action column of the row you are defining in the Macro grid, then release the mouse button.

5. Access adds the appropriate action to the Action cell, and fills in the action argument with the name of the object you dragged. For example, if you selected the Customers table in step 4, Access displays OpenTable in the action cell. Access also changes the values in the Action Arguments at the bottom of the Macro window: The Table Name changes to Customers, the View changes to Datasheet, and the DataMode changes to Edit.

● **TIP** If you drag the name of a report to the Action column of the Macro grid, Access sets the View action argument to Print Preview, not Print.

To Add an Action to a Macro

To add an action to the *end* of a macro:

1. Select the first empty row at the end of the macro.

2. Click on the down-pointing arrow at the end of the field in the Action column, or press Alt-↓ to display the action options. Select the action you want.

3. Press Tab to move to the Comments column. Enter a description that explains what action the step takes.

4. The Action Arguments section of the screen displays a set of properties and conditions depending on the action selected in step 2. As you move between the arguments, Access displays explanatory text that suggests what should be entered.

To insert an action into the *middle* of a macro:

1. Select the row where you want the action to be inserted.

2. Click in the square to the left of the row. Access displays a solid left arrow and highlights the row.

3. Press Ins, or select Edit ➤ Insert Row from the main menu. Access inserts a blank row. The row originally at this location, and all subsequent rows, are shifted down one row.

4. Click on the down-pointing arrow at the end of the field in the Action column, or press Alt-↓ to display the action options. Select the action you want.

5. Press Tab to move to the Comments column. Enter a description that explains what action the step takes.

6. The Action Arguments section of the screen displays a
    set of properties and conditions depending on the action
    selected in step 4. As you move between the arguments,
    Access displays explanatory text that suggests what
    should be entered. Enter the values for these arguments
    as appropriate for the action you want to perform.

To Delete an Action in a Macro

To remove an action from an existing macro:

1. Select the row containing the action you want to delete.

2. Click in the square to the left of the row. Access displays a
    solid left arrow and highlights the row.

3. Press Del, or select Edit ➤ Delete Row from the main
    menu. Access deletes the row and moves all subsequent
    rows in the grid up one row.

To Move an Action in a Macro

To move an action in a macro to another location within the macro:

1. Select the row containing the action you want to move.

2. Click in the square to the left of the row. Access displays a
    solid left arrow and highlights the row.

3. Click on the left arrow and drag the selected row to the
    new row position in the Macro grid where you want the
    action to take place. The pointer changes to an arrow with
    a box attached at the bottom as you drag.

4. Release the mouse button. The action at the location, and
    all actions underneath, are shifted down one row.

To Edit a Macro

To modify an existing macro:

1. Open the Database window by pressing F11.

2. Select the Macro button. Access displays a list of macros and macro groups.

3. Select the macro you want to edit.

4. Select Design. Access opens the Macro Window, shown in Figure A.13 in the Appendix.

5. In the grid, make the changes you need by adding or modifying actions, comments, or action arguments. See *To Create a Macro* for more information.

6. To save the macro, select File ➤ Save from the main menu. To save the macro under a new name, select File ➤ Save As and enter the new macro name.

To Copy a Macro

To make a copy of a macro or macro group:

1. Open the Database window by pressing F11.

2. Select the Macro button.

3. Select the name of the macro you want to copy.

4. Press Ctrl-C, or select Edit ➤ Copy from the main menu.

5. Select Edit ➤ Paste. Enter the name of the macro copy in the Macro Name field of the Paste As dialog box, then select OK.

To Delete a Macro or Macro Group

To delete a single macro or a macro group:

1. Open the Database window by pressing F11.

2. Select the Macro button.

3. Select the name of the macro you want to delete.

4. Press Del or select Edit ➤ Delete from the main menu.

5. Access asks you to confirm your request. Click on OK to delete the macro or on Cancel to return to the Database window.

To Delete a Macro in a Macro Group

To delete a macro contained in a macro group:

1. Open the Database window by pressing F11.

2. Select the Macro button.

3. Select the name of the macro group, then select Design.

4. Select the row that contains the macro by clicking on the box to the left of the Macro Name column. Access displays the row in reverse video. If the macro you want to delete is longer than one row, select the first row and drag the mouse down so that all rows are selected.

5. Press Del or select Edit ➤ Delete from the main menu.

6. Access asks you to confirm your request. Click on OK to delete the macro or on Cancel to return to the Database window.

To Run an Entire Macro

You can run a macro from the Database window or from the macro's Design view.

To run a macro from the Database window

You can start a macro from the Database window. To run the macro:

1. Open the Database window by pressing F11.

2. Select the macro button.

3. Select the macro you want to run.

- If you choose to run a macro group, enter the macro group name, a period, and the macro name (for example, **macrogroup.opencustomers**). Otherwise Access runs the *first* macro defined in the macro group.

4. Double-click on the macro name or press the Run button.

To run a macro from the macro's Design view

You can run a macro from Design view in two ways. Select the macro you want to run, or select the macro within a macro that you want to run, then:

1. Click on the Run button in the tool bar (the third button from the left, with a large exclamation point [!]).

2. Select Macro ➤ Run from the main menu.

To run a macro from other locations within Access

You can run a macro when you are working with forms, reports, and designs of other Access objects:

1. Select File ➤ Run Macro from the main menu.

2. Access displays the Macro Name box. Select the name of the macro you want to run.

   • If you choose to run a macro group, enter the macro group name, a period, and the macro name (for example, **macrogroup.opencustomers**). Otherwise Access runs the *first* macro defined in the macro group.

3. Select OK.

To Single-Step through a Macro

To run a macro one step at a time from the macro's Design view:

1. Click on the Single Step button in the tool bar (the fourth button from the left, with a shoe print), or select Macro ➤ Single Step from the main menu.

2. Click on the Run button in the tool bar (the third button from the left, with a large exclamation point [!]). Alternatively, select Macro ➤ Run from the main menu.

3. Access displays the Macro Single Step dialog box, which displays the macro name, the action it is performing, and the arguments for the action.

4. Select Step to execute the next action. Select Continue to execute the next and all subsequent actions without single-stepping through each action. Select Halt to stop the macro and remove the Macro Single Step window.

To Create a Macro Group

A macro group consists of one or more macros saved in a single macro file. To create a macro group:

1. Create a new macro by following steps 1 through 7 of *To Create a Macro* (above) but do *not* save the macro.

2. Click on the Macro Names button (the first button in the tool bar). Access adds a column named Macro Name to the grid.

3. Type the name of the macro in the Macro Name column of the first row (the row that contains the macro's first action). This is the same column used to assign a shortcut key or key combination to a macro.

4. If you want to add another macro to the macro group, move to the next blank row and create another macro. Enter a name for the macro in the Macro Name column of the row that contains the macro's first action. Repeat this step until all macros have been added. (You can modify a macro group and add, change, or delete individual macros within a macro group later.)

5. Save the macro group by selecting File ➤ Save from the main menu. Enter the name of the macro group in the Macro Name box. This saves the macro *group* as a single macro object (the individual macros are *not* saved separately and are not listed separately in the Macro list in the Database window).

● **TIP**   To run a macro from a macro group, such as from a command button or by using the File ➤ Run Macro command from the main menu, enter the macro group name, a period, and the macro name. For example, to run the *opencustomers* macro from the macro group named *macrogroup*, enter **macrogroup.opencustomers**. If you use only the macro group name, Access runs the *first* macro defined in the macro group.

To Debug a Macro

To find a problem in a macro, single-step through the execution of the macro. When the macro encounters a problem, an Action Failed dialog box appears and displays the action that caused the error. Press the Halt key to stop the macro, then correct the macro action that triggered the error.

To Set Macro Conditions

If you need to execute a macro only if a condition is true (for example, if a numeric value in a field is over a maximum value), you can specify a macro condition.

A condition is similar to a criterion used in a query grid. A condition, such as Taxable = Yes, evaluates to true or false. If the condition evaluates to true, the action in the macro is taken. If the condition evaluates to false, Access does not perform the action.

1. Click on the Conditions button in the tool bar (illustrated on the inside front cover), or select View ➤ Conditions from the main menu.

2. Access displays a new column called Condition on the grid.

3. Enter the condition you want evaluated. If the condition involves a field on the current form (the form the macro is working on), you need only specify the field name. If the condition involves a control (field) on a different form, enter the control name in the condition as *Forms! formname!controlname*.

4. If you want two or more actions to be taken if a condition evaluates to true, enter an ellipsis (three dots) in the second (and succeeding) cells in the Condition column.

To Assign a Macro to a Control on a Form

To assign a macro to a control on a form so Access will execute the macro when Access events occur, such as when you push a button or when a field becomes current (the cursor enters a field):

1. Display the form in Design view. See *Design View* for more information.

2. Select the control.

3. Enter the macro name in one of the properties listed in the table below. If the macro is part of a macro group, enter the group name, a period, and the macro name in the On-Push property.

Property	When macro runs
AfterUpdate	After data in control is saved
BeforeUpdate	Before data in control is saved
OnDblClick	When user double-clicks the control
OnEnter	Before moving to this control (such as with Tab)
OnExit	Before user leaves the control
OnPush	When user clicks the control (if control is a button)

Assigning Macros to Forms

You can assign a macro to a button on a form. When you click on the button in Form view, Access will execute the actions defined in the macro.

1. Display the form in Design view. See *Design View* for more information.

2. Select View ➤ Properties from the main menu or click on the Properties button in the tool bar (illustrated on the inside front cover).

3. Enter the macro name in one of the properties listed in the table below. If the macro is part of a macro group, enter the macro group name, a period, and the macro name in the On Push property cell.

Property	When macro runs
AfterUpdate	After saving the current record
BeforeUpdate	Before saving the current record
OnClose	Before closing the form
OnCurrent	Before displaying a record (either the first record if the form is being opened, or different record if form is already opened)
OnDelete	Before deleting the current record
OnInsert	Before inserting a new record
OnOpen	Before opening the form

See Also *Using the Keyboard in Access* in Part II

MAILING LABELS

Mailing labels can be used to create address labels for letters or any other type of label you need (such as labels for the cover of a report).

To Create Mailing Labels

In Access, mailing labels are a special type of report. To create mailing labels:

1. Open the Database window by pressing F11.

2. Select the Report button.

3. Select New.

4. Access displays the New Report dialog box. Select the table or query that contains the fields you want on the mailing label. Click on the down-pointing arrow key or press Alt-↓, then select the table or query name.

5. Select the ReportWizards button.

6. The ReportWizard displays the types of reports available. Select Mailing Labels from the list, then select OK.

7. Select from the Available fields list the field to appear on the first line of the report . Click on the > button. The ReportWizard screen is shown in Figure III.17.

8. Enter a special character or another field for the same line, if any.

- To enter a special character (a colon, comma, dash, period, or slash), click on the corresponding button below the Available fields list.

- To enter a space, click on the Space button.

- To enter custom text, such as **TO:**, enter the text in the box to the left of the Text-> button, then click on the Text-> button to add the custom text to the label.

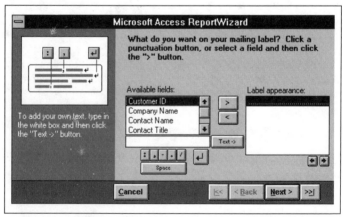

Figure III.17: The ReportWizard lets you select fields to include on mailing labels.

9. To begin a new line, click on the new line button.

10. To remove characters or a field from the Label appearance list, click on the < button. Fields and characters are removed one at a time each time you click on the < button.

11. Repeat steps 7 through 10 as many times as needed to build your label.

12. When the label is complete, click the Next> button.

13. The ReportWizard asks you which field you want to sort on. With mailing labels you may wish to sort on the zip or postal code. Select the field from the Available fields list and press the > button; the field is moved to the Sort order list.

- To remove a field from the Sort Order list, click on the < button. To select all fields, click on the >> button.

- To remove all fields from the sort order list, click on the << button.

14. Select the Next> button.

15. Select the label size you want. The ReportWizard lists the Avery label number, a label's dimensions, and the number of labels across. Select the Next> button.

16. Select Print Preview to see a sample label, or select Design view to further refine the label layout.

NULL

A field has a null value if no entry has been made in the field. For example, if you skip a numeric field during data entry, it contains a value of null rather than 0.

You can use the null value in queries and conditions in macros to check if a field has data in it. For example, in the conditions cell of a query, you can use the expression **Is Null** to include or exclude records in which the field contains no data.

See Also *Expressions*

ONE-TO-MANY RELATIONSHIP

In a one-to-many relationship between tables, a table is related to another table through a common field. For example, a customer table can be related to an orders table if both tables contain a field in which the customer number is stored. In a one-to-many relationship, the "one" side (the customer table) is related to one or more records on the "many" side (the orders table). In fact, the table on the "one side" may have no records in the "many" table. Thus, a customer record may have no orders.

One-to-many relationships are created by joining tables.

See Also *Joining Tables; One-to-One Relationship*

ONE-TO-ONE RELATIONSHIP

In a one-to-one relationship between tables, a record in a table has *only one* related record in another table. A one-to-one relationship is established by joining tables.

See Also *Joining Tables; One-to-Many Relationship*

OPTION GROUPS

An option group is a set of buttons, check boxes, or toggle buttons of which only one can be "on" or "true". Each object in an option group has its own OptionValue property. The OptionValue is returned by Access when you select the object in the group. For example, in a group of three buttons, selecting the first button could return 1, selecting the second button could return 2, and so on.

You create option groups by first creating a group frame, which is bound to a field or set to an expression. An option group can also be unbound.

To Create an Option Group

To combine a set of controls into an option group:

1. Open the form in Design view. See *Design View* for more information.

2. Select the option group tool from the toolbox (illustrated on the inside front cover).

3. To create an option group bound to a field, select the field from the Field window and drag the field name to the form. This sets the ControlSource property of the option group to the field name. The field type should be Yes/No, Integer, or Long Integer for best results. Go to step 5.

4. To create an unbound option group, click on the form where you want the option group to appear. You must manually set the expression within the ControlSource property for the option group.

5. Select the type of control you want to use within the option group: choose the check box, option button, or toggle button from the toolbox.

6. Click inside the option group at the position of the upper-left corner where you want the first control to appear. The group control changes to reverse video as soon as the pointer moves into it. Access places the first control in the option group. Repeat this step until you have the number of controls you need in the option group.

7. Set the OptionValue property for each control within the group.

See Also *Controls*

OUTER JOIN

When tables are joined together in an outer join, Access queries display all records in the primary table whether or not they have related records in the related table.

See Also *Joining Tables; One-to-Many Relationship; Referential Integrity*

PAGE BREAKS

Page breaks can be used to start a new screen for a multiscreen form. Page breaks can also be used to enforce a page break at a selected point on a form when you print a report.

To Create a Multiscreen Form

You can use page breaks to instruct Access to break a long form into several pages. When you use the form in data entry mode, press Page Down and Page Up to move between screens.

To create a form that spans more than one screen:

1. Open the form in Design view. See *Design View* for more information.

2. Open the toolbox if it is not displayed: press View ➤ Toolbox from the main menu.

3. Select the Page Break tool (illustrated on the inside front cover). Click at the point on the form where you want the new screen to begin. Access displays a short dashed horizontal line at the left side of the form where the page break occurs.

To Create a Page Break in a Report

The page break control in the toolbox forces Access to begin a new page at a specified location. To add a page break to a report form:

1. Open the report in Design view. See *Design View* for more information.

2. Open the toolbox if it is not displayed: press View ➤ Toolbox from the main menu.

3. Select the Page Break tool (illustrated on the inside back cover). Click at the location on the report where you want the new screen to begin, in a detail section, or in the header or footer section of a control break. Access displays a short dashed horizontal line at the left side of the report where the page break occurs.

PAGE FOOTERS

See *Headers and Footers*

PAGE HEADERS

See *Headers and Footers*

PAGE NUMBERS

You can add a page number to a report by adding a text box with an expression that contains a variation of the Page function as follows:

1. Open the report in Design view. See *Design View* for more information.

2. Select the Report button.

3. Select Design.

4. If the toolbox is not displayed, open it by selecting View ➤ Toolbox. The toolbox is illustrated on the inside front cover.

5. If the Page Footer section is large enough to contain the page number field, go to step 6. Otherwise, expand the Page Footer section: move the pointer to the bottom portion of the footer so that it changes to a double-pointed arrow. Drag the pointer down to expand the size of the footer.

6. Click on the text box button in the toolbox. Move the pointer to the Page Footer section.

7. Click in the upper-left corner of the area in which you want the text box to appear, then drag to the lower-right corner of the text box. Release the mouse button, then drag the box or resize it if you wish.

8. Click inside the text box. Enter **=Page** and click anywhere outside the box. This will display the number 1 in the text box area on the report on page 1, the number 2 on page 2, and so on.

9. Click outside the text box.

• **TIP**   You can make page numbers more explicit. Use any of the following expressions instead of =Page in step 8 above:

Expression	What the report will print
="Page " & Page	Page 1, Page 2, etc.
="-" & Page & "-"	-1-, -2-, etc.
="Page " & Format(Page, "000")	Page 001, Page 002, etc.

Alternatively, you can enter the page expression in the Properties window. If the Properties window is not open, click on the Properties button in the tool bar or select View ➤ Properties from the main menu. In the Control Source property, enter the expression you want. Always be sure to begin the expression with an equal sign (=).

See Also   *Sections*

PARADOX

Access can use data stored in a Paradox formatted file. Similarly, data stored in Access can be saved in Paradox format for use in other applications.

To Save a Table in Paradox Format

To save an existing Access table as a Paradox table:

1.   Close the table. If you are working in a multiuser environment, all users must close the table.

2.   Open the Database window by pressing F11.

3.   Select File ➤ Export from the main menu.

4.   In the Data Destination text box, select Paradox, then select OK.

5.   From the list of tables in the current database, select the table you want to export, then select OK.

6.   Enter the name of the file you want to export *to*. Access adds the .DB file extension for you if necessary.

7.   Access adjusts field names if they are too long or do not conform to Paradox standards.

To Attach or Import an Existing Paradox Table

To attach or import a file from a Paradox database:

1.   Be sure the Microsoft Access database that will contain the Paradox database is open.

2.   Select File ➤ Attach Table from the main menu to attach a Paradox file; select File ➤ Import to import a Paradox file.

3.   Select Paradox as the Data Source.

4.   Select the Paradox file you want to use. Paradox files have the .DB extension.

5.   If the Paradox table was encrypted when it was saved in Paradox, Access prompts you for the password. Enter the password and select OK.

Access converts the following Paradox data types to those that Access can use:

Paradox type	Access type (FieldSize Property)
Alphanumeric	Text
Currency	Number (Double)
Date	Date/Time
Number	Number (Double)
Short Number	Number (Integer)

PARAMETER QUERIES

A parameter query allows you to run a query repeatedly but change a value each time you run it. A parameter query prompts you for the criteria you want to use when you run the query. Parameter queries eliminate the need to create queries that are identical except for a value in the criteria.

To Create a Parameter Query

To create a query that prompts you for a criteria value:

1. Create a select query (the standard type of query).

2. In the criteria row of the QBE grid, press [, type the text prompt you want displayed when you run the query, then press].

3. Select Query ➤ Parameters from the main menu. Access displays the Query Parameters dialog box (see Figure III.18).

4. In the Parameter box, enter the *identical* prompt text you entered in step 2. Do *not* include the square brackets ([and]).

5. In the Data Type box, select the data type of the field you will be entering when Access displays the prompt. Select OK.

6. Run the query. Access displays an Enter Parameter Value dialog box containing your prompt and provides an area for you to enter the value. When you have entered the criteria value, press OK.

See Also   *Select Queries; Action Queries; Queries*

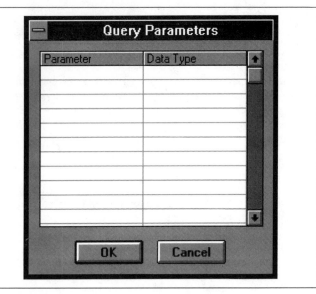

Figure III.18: The Query Parameters dialog box

PASSWORDS

Access allows you to add, change, or delete passwords. If a user forgets a password, a member of the Admins group must clear the password. See *User and Group Accounts* for more information on the Admins group.

To Add a Password

To add a password for a user:

1. Display the Database by pressing F11.

2. Select Security ➤ Change Password from the main menu. Access displays the Change Password dialog box, shown in Figure III.19.

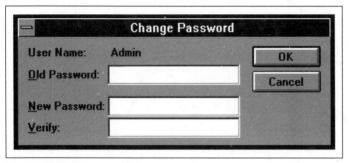

Figure III.19: The Change Password dialog box

3. Enter the new password in the New Password box.

4. Enter the *same* password entered in step 4 in the Verify box.

   - The text must match character for character.

   - Access passwords are case sensitive: *ABC* does not match *abc*.

5. Click on OK to make the change, or press Cancel to leave the password unchanged.

6. If the passwords in the New Password and Verify boxes do not match, Access asks you to re-enter the password in the Verify box. If the passwords still do not match, press Cancel and begin again at step 2.

To Change a Password

To modify an existing password:

1. Display the Database by pressing F11.

2. Select Security ➤ Change Password from the main menu.

3. Enter the existing password in the Old Password box.

4. Enter the new password in the New Password box.

5. Enter the *same* password entered in step 4 in the Verify box.

  • The text must match character for character.

  • Access passwords are case sensitive: *ABC* does not match *abc*.

6. Click on OK to make the change, or press Cancel to leave the password unchanged.

7. If the passwords in the New Password and Verify boxes do not match, Access asks you to re-enter the password in the Verify box. If the passwords still do not match, press Cancel and begin again at step 2.

To Clear a User Password

To clear an existing user password:

1. Open the Database window by pressing F11.

2. Select Security ➤ Users from the main menu.

3. Enter the user account name in the Name box, or select the user account name from the drop-down list.

4. Select Clear Password.

To Log On to Access Using a Password

If you have established security with Access, Access displays a Logon screen when you start the program.

To log on to a secure Access system:

1. Enter your user name in the Name box.

2. Enter your password in the Password box. If you do not have a password assigned, leave the box blank—do *not* enter spaces.

3. Select OK.

See Also   *User and Group Accounts; Permissions*

PERMISSIONS

Permissions determine which users and groups can have read and write authority to a database object. You need to specify three parts to Access to determine permission:

- The object for which permission will be granted

- The user and group name that will be affected by the permission

- The type of permission you are granting

To Assign Permissions to Users and Groups

To assign permission to a user or group:

1. Open the Database window by pressing F11.

2. Select Security ➤ Permissions from the main menu. Access displays the Permissions dialog box, shown in Figure III.20.

3. Select the object Type and Name from the Object section of the dialog box. Enter the Type and Name directly or select it from the pull-down list.

4. Select either the Users button or the Groups button in the User/Group List option. Select the User or Group you want to grant permission to for this object.

5. Select the type of permissions to grant to the user or group for the specified object. If an X appears in the permission option check box, the permission is granted; if the option's check box is empty, permission is not granted. Select any of the following permission options:

Read Definitions allows the user or group to view but not change the object.

Modify Definitions allows the user or group to modify the object.

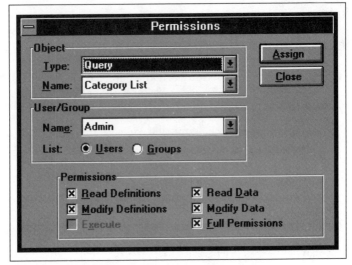

Figure III.20: The Permissions dialog box

Execute allows the user or group to run a form or report object and generate data, or execute a macro object.

Read Data allows the user or group to view data in a table or query, and allows the user or group to run an action query (action queries update database tables).

Modify Data allows the user or group to view and modify data in a table or query.

Full Permissions allows the user or group to do anything within Access.

6. Select Assign to add the permissions.

To Change Permissions to Users and Groups

To change a permission already assigned to a user or group:

1. Open the Database window by pressing F11.

2. Select Security ➤ Permissions from the main menu. Access displays the Permissions dialog box shown in Figure III.20.

3. Select the object Type and Name from the Object section of the dialog box. Enter the Type and Name directly or select them from the pull-down list.

4. Select either the Users button or the Groups button in the User/Group List option. Select the User or Group you want to grant permission to for this object.

5. Access displays the permissions that already exist for the object and user/group combination. Select the type of permissions you want to grant to the user or group for the specified object. If an X appears in the permission option check box, the permission is granted; if the option's check box is empty, permission is not granted. The permission options are listed in *To Assign Permissions to Users and Groups* above.

6. Select Assign to change the permissions.

PICTURES

See *Graphics*

PRIMARY KEY

A primary key is a field or group of fields that identifies a record in a table. No two records in a table can have the same primary key.

While a primary key is not required, primary keys are used as indexes to a table, they significantly speed up Access when it searches for values in a table.

To Set the Primary Key

To create the primary key in a table:

1. Open a table in Design view. See *Design View* for more information.

2. Click in the box to the left of the field name of the row containing the field you want to use as the primary key. Access will display the row in reverse video. To select more than one field, hold down Ctrl while you select each row.

3. Select the Primary Key button from the tool bar (the button that shows a key), or select Edit ➤ Set Primary Key from the main menu. Access displays a key symbol to the left of the field name.

● **TIP**   If you do not specify a key when you save a table's design, Access asks if you want it to create a primary key for you. If you select Yes, Access adds a field to your table and defines it with a Counter data type. Fields with a Counter data type are numbered beginning with the value 1, and automatically incremented by Access when you add new records. You cannot change the value in a field with a Counter data type.

● **TIP**   When you define a relationship between two tables, Access first looks at the primary key for each table and suggests that this field be used to join the two tables. Therefore, if the table will be used in relationships with other tables, select the common field (the field used to join the two tables) as the primary key.

To Change the Primary Key

To change the primary key in a table:

1. Open a table in Design view. See *Design View* for more information.

2. Click in the box to the left of the field name of the row containing the field you want to use as the primary key.

Access will display the row in reverse video. To select
more than one field, hold down Ctrl while you select
each row.

3.   Select the Primary Key button from the tool bar (the button that shows a key), or Select Edit ➤ Set Primary Key
from the main menu. Access displays a key symbol to the
left of the field name, and removes the key symbol from
fields (rows) that are no longer part of the primary key.

To Delete the Primary Key

To remove the primary key from a table:

1.   Open in Design view the table that contains the key you
want to remove. See *Design View* for more information.

2.   Open the Properties window by clicking on the Properties button in the tool bar (illustrated on the inside back
cover), or select View ➤ Table Properties from the main
menu.

3.   Press Tab or ↓ to move to the cell to the right of *Primary
Key*, then press Del. Alternatively, click directly in the
property cell, highlight the entry, and press Del.

See Also   *Index*

PRINTING

Access provides an easy way to print all the data you have worked
with, whether in Form, Report, or Datasheet view. You cannot,
however, print an object from within Design view.

To Print an Object

To print data in a form, report, or datasheet:

1.   Select File ➤ Print from the main menu.

2. Access asks you to specify the print range and number of copies, and may ask you to select the print quality, depending on the printer you are using. Select the settings you want.

- To select the printer, page orientation, paper size, or margins, select Setup, select the settings, and select OK.

3. Select OK to print the object, or select Cancel to return to the object's view without printing it.

4. Access prints your object and shows its progress in a window in the middle of your screen.

To Preview the Printing of an Object

To look at the layout of a printed object before the object is actually printed:

1. Select File ➤ Print Preview from the main menu, or click on the Print Preview button. This button shows a magnifying glass over a sheet of paper.

2. Select one of the following:

- Select Print to print the object. This is the equivalent of selecting File ➤ Print from the main menu.
- Select Setup to select the printer, margins, paper orientation, and paper size.
- Select Zoom to display the preview screen in a larger font. Select Zoom again to return to full-screen view.
- Select Cancel to return to the object without printing.

PROPERTIES

Properties dictate the behavior or specify the features and characteristics of a form or report, or the controls on these objects on a form. For example, controls have a default value property, a color property, and a height property.

Properties can be set by using design tools (such as the Palette window), or by entering or selecting the property value directly in a cell in the Properties window.

To Set a Property

To set a property for an Access object:

1. Open a form or report in Design view. See *Design View* for more information.

2. Select the object whose property or properties you want to change.

3. If the Properties window is not displayed, select the Properties button on the tool bar (illustrated on the inside front cover), or select View ➤ Properties from the main menu. The Properties window is shown in Figure III.21.

4. Click in the cell to the right of the property you want to change, or press ↓ or Tab until you reach this cell. If you go too far, press ↑ or Shift-Tab to go back.

5. If the property values are limited, Access displays a down-pointing arrow at the right side of the cell. Click on this arrow or press Alt-↓ to display the valid options, then select the option you want. Go to step 7.

6. If the property value is not restricted, enter the value of the property in the cell.

7. Click in another property cell or anywhere outside the property box to make the property value permanent.

QUERIES

The Find feature in Access searches for values within a field, searching and displaying one record at a time.

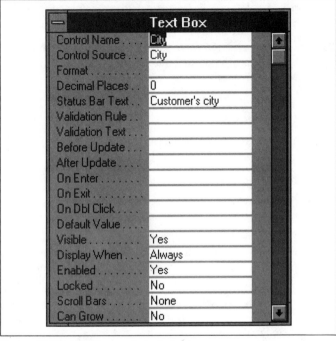

Figure III.21: The Properties window

Queries are used to find more than one record. In addition, queries let you specify the fields you want to see in the Datasheet, as well as the order of the fields. You can also sort records and specify critieria to limit which records are displayed.

Records can be displayed in Datasheet view, the spreadsheet-like layout used in other areas of Access, shown in Figure A.5 in the Appendix. As with other grids, you can move columns, change the width of columns or height of rows, and insert columns.

To run a query you must tell Access two things:

- which fields you want to display
- which field contains the values you want to look for or limit the search to; for example, you might want to see only records that contain *Canada* in the Country field.

When you execute a query, Access finds the records you requested and displays them. This set of records is called a *dynaset*—a set of records that is created dynamically. The dynaset is simply a subset of the records from the complete table. Unlike other database programs that create a subset for display only, Access lets you add, edit, or delete records from the Datasheet view of the dynaset.

With the records in Datasheet view, you can:

- Change the query by clicking on the Design button or selecting View ➤ Query Design from the main menu.

- Find a particular value within any of the columns by clicking on the Find button (the button with the binoculars) or selecting Edit ➤ Find from the main menu.

- Change the layout of the Datasheet: change the font, column order, column width, and so on.

- Save your changes in Design view for future use by selecting File ➤ Save As and enter a *new* query name.

In fact, you can even create a new data entry form to display the records in a custom layout by clicking on the New form button on the tool bar.

To Create a New Query

To design a new query:

1. Open the Database window by pressing F11.

2. Select the Query button.

3. Select the New button.

4. Use ↑ and ↓ to highlight the table you want to use, then press Enter. You can select the table directly by double-clicking on the table or query the new query is based on.

5. Repeat step 4 for each table that contains information you will use in your query. Select Close when you have selected all the tables.

6. Access displays the Select Query window shown in Figure A.5 in the Appendix. Notice that at the top of the window Access displays a window listing all fields in a table; Access displays a window for each table you selected in steps 4 and 5. Key fields are displayed in boldface. At the bottom of the Select Query window is another grid, called the Query by Example grid, or QBE grid for short, which holds the criteria.

7. In the first column of the QBE grid, specify the name of the first field you want to see in the resulting Datasheet. The insertion point is blinking in the first cell of the first column of the QBE grid, which is where the field name must be placed. You can select the field in one of two ways:

- Click the down-pointing arrow in the cell or press Alt-↓, highlight the field, and press enter.

- Click in the table field list window at the top of the window. Select the field name, and drag the field name to the first Field cell in the QBE grid. When the pointer points to the Field cell, it changes into a rectangle, indicating that Access is ready to drop the field name into the cell.

8. Repeat step 7 for each field you want to display. Alternatively, if you want to display all fields from a table, you can use one of two shortcuts:

- Select the first field listed in the table's field list; the field is noted by an asterisk (*). Drag the asterisk to the QBE grid. The * is shorthand for displaying all fields in the Datasheet. If you want to enter criteria for any of the fields, you must use an additional column and specify the field. To suppress the field's display a second time (the field is displayed as part of the * designator), click in the Show row so that an X does not appear.

- Double-click on the field list window's title, then click and drag to the first available row in the QBE grid. Access fills in each field from the table into a separate column in the QBE grid. To enter criteria, select the field's column and enter the criteria in the Criteria row.

9.   Press Tab or click in the Field cell of the second column. Repeat steps 7 and 8 until all fields you want to display are included in the QBE grid.

10.   If you want to enter criteria for any of the fields already selected, use the Criteria cell of the column corresponding to this field. Otherwise, add the field to a new column in the QBE grid.

11.   Enter the criteria. In the *Criteria* row, enter the expression Access should use to evaluate whether it should include or exclude a record. See *Expressions* for more information about the form of the criteria.

12.   Run the Query. See *To Run a Query* below.

● **TIP**   If you are using joined tables, select the field from the table you want to use. Access does not display the name of the table that contains the field. To obtain the table name for each field, view the SQL query that is generated. Select View ➤ SQL from the main menu. In the SQL Text box, Access displays each field selected in *formname.[fieldname]* format.

See Also   *Layering Access Objects*

To Run a Query

If you have a query defined and open in Design view, you can run the query by one of these three methods:

*   Click on the Datasheet button in the tool bar (the second button from the left).

*   Click on the Run button (the fifth button from the left, with a large exclamation point [!]).

*   Select View ➤ Datasheet.

Access creates the dynaset and displays the records in a Datasheet.

To run the query from the Database window:

1.   Click on the Query button.

2.   Select the query you want to run.

3.   Double-click on the query name or select Open.

● **TIP**   To stop the execution of a query, press Ctrl-Break.

To Save a Query

To save a query design for future use:

1.   If the Query is in Query view, select File ➤ Save Query.
(If you have the Query open in Design view, select
File ➤ Save.)

2.   If the query is new and has not been saved, Access asks
you to name it. Enter the query name and select OK.

To Save a Query Using a Different Name

To keep a copy of a modified query separate from the original
query, select File ➤ Save As (in Design view) or File ➤ Save
Query As (in Datasheet view). Enter the new query name and
select OK.

To Close a Query

Select File ➤ Close or double-click on the control box in the upper-
left corner of the Query to return to the Database window.

● **TIP**   To see the name of the table in the QBE grid, select View
➤ Table Names from the main menu. Access adds another row to
the QBE grid and displays the table that contains the field.

● **TIP**   You can create a simple query that includes all fields from
all joined tables in a dynaset, which is useful as the basis for other
queries or reports. Select View ➤ Query Properties from the main
menu. Remove the X from the Restrict Available Fields check box
and select OK.

Adding Another Related Table to a Query

To add another table to a query:

1. Display the query in Design view. (Click on the Design button or select View ➤ Query Design.) See *Design View* for more information.

2. Select Query ➤ Add Table from the main menu. The Add Table dialog box, shown in Figure III.22, is displayed.

3. Select the table you want to add from the Table/Query list. Select Add, then select Close.

4. Since Access already knows about the relationship for these two tables, it displays a line between the related fields. If not, you can create the relationship by highlighting a field in one table and dragging it to the related field in another table.

5. Click on the Datasheet or Run button on the tool bar (illustrated on the inside front cover), or select View ➤ Datasheet from the main menu.

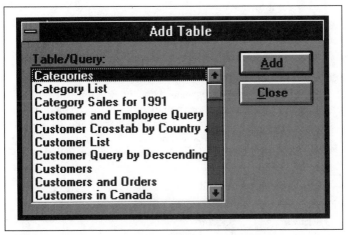

Figure III.22: The Add Table dialog box

Figure A.16 in the Appendix shows a query with a set of joined tables.

● **TIP**   You can use drag-and-drop to add another table to a query. With the query in Design view, press F11 to open the Database window. Click on the Table button, then select the table name from the list. Select Window ➤ Tile from the main menu. Drag the table to the query form. Access adds another field window for the table you selected.

To Use a Query to Perform Calculations

You can use a query to group fields and calculate totals, averages, and other standard arithmetic calculations. To use this feature, you must display the Total: row in the QBE grid, then select the type of calculation you want to make (called an *aggregate function*).

Aggregate functions perform a calculation on a group (aggregate) of records. Aggregate functions include calculating an average or finding the largest or smallest value in a table or query.

1. Open a select query in Design view. See *Design View* for more information.

2. If the *Total:* row is not displayed in the QBE grid, click on the Totals button on the tool bar, or select View ➤ Totals from the main menu. The tool bar is shown on the inside front cover.

3. Build a select query as usual: Drag the field on which you want to use a calculation to the QBE grid. In the Total row click on the down-pointing arrow, or press Alt-↓. Select from one of the aggregate functions listed below. Aggregate functions specify the type of calculation you want to make.

4. Run the query.

Access uses the following aggregate functions:

Function	Used to
Avg	Compute the average value
Count	Count the number of values

Function	Used to
Expression	Evaluate an expression for this field
First	Display the value in the first record (using the current sort order)
Group By	The default setting; this performs no calculation
Last	Display the value in the last record (using the current sort order)
Max	Find the largest (maximum) value
Min	Find the smallest (minimum) value
StDev	Compute the standard deviation
Sum	Add all values
Var	Compute the variance of all values
Where	Restrict records in a crosstab. (Where specifies a limiting expression; fields that use the Where value are not displayed.)

● **TIP** To use a criterion to control which values resulting from a calculation are displayed, include a criteria expression in the same column as the aggregate function. Access performs the aggregate function, then compares the result with the criteria to determine if it should display the record.

To limit which records are included in the records used in an aggregate function before it is executed, use the Where function. If you use an expression in the Field row and the Where option in the Total row, Access evaluates the Where expression for a record to determine if the record should be included in any calculations. Fields that use the Where function are not displayed in a query; the Where function allows you to use additional criteria to limit which records are included in a query.

See Also *Columns; Crosstabs; Filters; Sort Order*

READ-ONLY FILES

Using read-only mode, you can allow a user to view but not modify data in a database.

To Open a Database in Read-Only Mode

To open a database so that a user can view but not change the data in a database:

1. Select File ➤ Open Database from the main menu.

2. Select the drive, directory, and file name of the database you want to open.

3. If an *X* does not appear in the Read Only box of the Open Database dialog box, click on the box or press Alt-R.

4. Select OK.

RECORD LOCKING

Record locking options are set in the Custom Multiuser Options.

See Also *Current Record Indicators; Customizing Access*

RECORDS

A record contains all the data about a subject, such as information about an order, a customer, or an invoice. A table consists of many records. You can add, delete, and modify records using a datasheet or form view. Records, in turn, are made up of fields.

Information about adding and deleting records can be found in *Datasheets* and *Forms*.

● **TIP**   To display the most current record information in a form or report, which is useful in a multiuser environment, select Records ➤ Refresh from the main menu.

See Also   *Datasheets; Forms; Tables; Queries*

RECTANGLES

To draw a rectangle on a form or report, follow the directions for drawing lines (see *Lines*) but select the rectangle tool instead of the line tool.

See Also   *Drawing Tools*

REFERENTIAL INTEGRITY

Referential integrity controls how your records are maintained when tables are joined. Referential integrity stops you from deleting a record in the primary table if it has a related record in the related table.

To enable referential integrity:

1.   Open the Database window by pressing F11.

2.   Select Edit ➤ Relationships from the main menu.

3.   Enter the primary and secondary table names.

4.   Click on the Enforce Referential Integrity box so that an *X* appears in it.

Use Referential Integrity to keep joined tables in sync.

See Also   *Joining Tables*

REPORTS

Reports allow you to present your data in print, or send your data to disk for printing by someone else or at another computer. You can create reports to list individual records in sorted order, show records grouped by a field value, or summarize data. For example, you can list all customers alphabetically, print all customers by state, or count the number of customers by country.

As with forms, Access provides a Wizard, called the ReportWizard, to simplify creating reports.

Reports share many features seen in queries: You can save a report and run it again. You can design a report so that it uses the results of a query rather than all records in a table. If you need to report on a subset of records from a table, a query is an efficient screening mechanism that improves the performance of the report feature of Access. This speeds up creating reports because queries are more efficient at selecting records than are reports.

To Create a Single-Column Report

To create a report in which all selected fields are displayed in a column:

1. Open the Database window by pressing F11.
2. Select the Report button.
3. Select the New button.
4. Access needs to know which table or query you want to work with. Click on the down-pointing arrow key to display the list of available tables and queries, or press Alt-↓. Use ↑ and ↓ and highlight the table or query, then press Enter.

- You can select the table or query directly by double-clicking on the table or query name in the list box.

- Alternatively, enter the name of the table or query in the Select a Table/Query box.

5. Select the ReportWizard button. Access now asks a series of questions.

6. Access first asks what style of report you want. A single-column report lists one record per line, with fields placed vertically, one above another. A Groups/Totals report allows you to sort and list fields by a field, then create subtotals when a field's value changes. Mailing Label reports create address labels for envelopes or other special purposes. Select Single-Column and select OK.

7. The ReportWizard asks which fields you want to include on the form. Highlight the first field you want included on the report. This field will appear first in the column on the report. Click on the > button. The field name is removed from the *Available fields* list and added to the *Field order on report* list. Similarly, add the other fields you want on the report. Select the Next> button.

8. The ReportWizard asks how you want to sort the data. Sort order refers to the alphabetical arrangement of the fields. Select the field you want to sort on first and click on the > button. The field name moves from the *Available fields* list to the *Sort order* list. Similarly, select the fields that will be sorted on next (secondary sorts). Click on the Next> button.

9. Select the look of the report. You can select any format, then view a sample in the magnifying glass at the left of the ReportWizard window. Select the Next> button.

10. Access asks for the report name. This name will appear in the Database window list when you select Reports. Enter the name of the report, then select the Print Preview button. Access launches the report and shows you a sample of the report.

11. Click on the Cancel button to display the report in Design view or on Print to print the report.

Figure A.12 in the Appendix shows a sample report in Design view.

See Also *Layering Access Objects*

To Create a Report Containing Groups

Reports can break down information by a field you designate as a group field. When the group changes, you can direct Access to display data in a Group Header on a report, print a total in a Group Footer, and do special formatting. You can sort a report on one or more group fields.

You can print summary subtotals and totals only and exclude detail records when you use a group report.

The most efficient way to create a group report is to use the Report-Wizard, then use its design as a basis for your own.

1. Begin in the Database window by pressing F11.

2. Select the Report button.

3. Select the New button.

4. Access needs to know which table or query you want to work with. Click on the down-pointing arrow key to display the list of available tables and queries, or press Alt-↓. Use ↑ and ↓ and highlight the table or query you want, then press Enter. You can select the table directly by double-clicking on the table or query name in the list box. (Alternatively, enter the name of the table or query in the Select a Table/Query box.)

5. Select the ReportWizard button.

6. Access asks what style of report you want. Select Groups/Totals and select OK.

7. The ReportWizard asks which fields you want to include on the form. Highlight the field you want as the primary (first) group heading and click on the > button. The field name moves from the *Available fields* list to the *Field order on report* list. *You must select the primary sorted field first.* Within this field you may want to have a secondary sort. If so, add the next field field to the *Field order on report* list next. Continue in this manner until all group fields are selected. Select the Next> button.

8.   The ReportWizard asks how to group the data. In most cases you want to keep the sort order the same as the order of the fields selected—that is, the first field selected is the primary sort field, the second field is the secondary sort field, and so on. The ReportWizard provides a shortcut: click on the >> button to select all fields in the *Available fields* list. Click on the Next> button.

9.   The ReportWizard asks how to group the data. Select Normal grouping. This tells Access to look at the entire contents of a field to see if a value in that field has changed.

10.   Select the look of the report. You can select any format, then view a sample in the magnifying glass at the left of the ReportWizard window. Select the Next> button.

11.   Access asks for the report name. This name will appear in the Database window list when you select Reports. Enter the report title and select the Print Preview button. This launches the report and shows you a sample of the report.

12.   Click on the Cancel button to display the report in Design view or on Print to print the report.

As with the single-column report, you can modify the report. Notice that the ReportWizard creates bands for each group field you selected, one for each grouping. The report contains a text field for the field heading in the first group header section, and another text field for the field heading in the second group header section.

To Use Snaking Columns on a Report

If your report contains more data than can fit in a single column, you can use a snaking column to wrap the text into the next column. To set up snaking columns:

1. Create a report and open it in Design view. See *Design View* for more information.

2. Select File ➤ Print Setup. Access displays a Print Setup dialog box.

3. Select the More button. Access opens the bottom of the Print Setup dialog box and displays more options. The dialog box is shown in Figure III.23.

4. Enter the number of columns you want in the Items Across box. Enter the amount of space you want between records in the Row Spacing box.

5. Enter the amount of space you want between columns in the Column Spacing box.

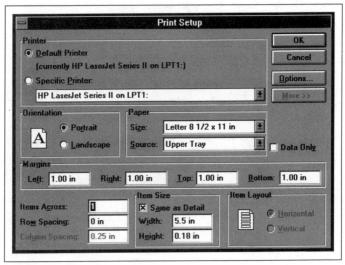

Figure III.23: The Print Setup dialog box

6. Select the Vertical option in the Item Layout section.

7. Select OK.

● **TIP**   If you have more text than will fit on a single line, set the field's Can Grow property to True. Access will use as many lines as necessary to print the entire contents of a field.

To Save a Report

To save a report design for future use:

1. Select File ➤ Save.

2. If this is the first time you have saved the report, Access asks you to name the report. Enter a name and select OK.

To Save a Report Using a Different Name

To keep a copy of a modified report separate from the original report, select File ➤ Save As. Enter the new report name and select OK.

To Copy an Existing Report

To make a copy of an existing report:

1. In the Database window, highlight the report and open it in Design view. See *Design View* for more information.

2. Select File ➤ Save As and enter the new report name.

To Close a Report

When you are done with a report and want to return to the Database window, select File ➤ Close. If you have made changes, Access asks if you want to save them. Select Yes to save the changes or No to discard them, then select Cancel to return to Design view.

REPORT SECTIONS

Reports in Access are *banded reports*—they have separate sections, each of which is identified by a band across the top. Standard reports created by the ReportWizard include a band for the report header, report detail, and a report footer.

By default, the FormWizard places the *=Now()* function in the Page Header. Now() displays your computer system's current date when the report is run. The Page Footer section created by a FormWizard contains a single control containing *=Page*. =Page is translated into a page number when the report is printed.

Figure A.12 in the Appendix shows a report with a Report Header, Page Header, Detail, and Page Footer section clearly displayed.

To View a Report with Data

To run the report and display a sample of the output on the screen before you print it:

1. Select File ➤ Sample Preview or File ➤ Print Preview from the main menu or click on the Print Preview button (the leftmost button in the tool bar).

2. Access displays the report, complete with data from your table or query. At the top of the preview window are four buttons: Print, Setup, Zoom, and Cancel.

3. To print the report from the Report Preview view, select the Print button.

4. To inspect or modify the printer settings, select the Setup button. Access displays a dialog box similiar to the Printer Setup dialog box in the Windows Control Panel or the Printer Setup options offered in most Windows applications.

5. To see a full page of the report, click on the Zoom button: click on it again to return to the close-up view.

6. Click on Cancel to return to Design view.

● **TIP** Use Sample Preview to look at the basic layout of a report, without extensive use of actual data. Sample Preview helps you verify alignment, font size and style, and other visual elements. Use Print Preview to look at the report with a complete set of actual data.

To Modify a Report

Working in a report's Design view is similar to working with a form in a Design view. You can click and drag controls to new locations or change their properties (for example, font and font size). As with forms, controls on a report are any of its elements, such as a picture, a field, or a report title.

See Also *Dates; Forms; Headers and Footers; Page Numbers; Grouping Data*

REPORTWIZARDS

See *Reports*

SECTIONS

See *Report Sections*

SECURITY

See *Passwords; User and Group Accounts*

SELECT QUERIES

By default, new queries are select queries. Select queries select records based on your criteria and display them in a form or datasheet. Other types of queries include action queries and parameter queries.

See Also *Action Queries; Parameter Queries; Queries*

SELF JOIN

See *Joining Tables*

SORT ORDER

When you set the sort order in a query, records in a dynaset are viewed in sorted order. You can sort a field in ascending order (0–9 and A–Z) or descending order (9–0 and Z–A) by choosing Ascending or Descending in the Sort: row in the QBE grid.

The datasheet is sorted by the first column in the QBE grid that contains a sort option (this field need not be the first column in the grid). If two records have the same value, Access looks at the next field to the right in the QBE grid that contains a sort option, looking to the columns.

You can remove the sorting option from a field by selecting *(not sorted)* in the Sort cell of the field you no longer want to sort.

● **TIP**   You need not specify each field in a query in order to sort on a single field. To include all fields in a query, drag the * field from the field window to the first Field cell in the QBE grid. Drag the field you want to sort on into the next column. Turn the Show option off (click in the box so the *X* disappears), then select the sort order you want. The dynaset will display all columns but sort on the field you specified.

SPREADSHEETS

Access can import and export data from a table to a spreadsheet that supports Lotus 1-2-3 or Microsoft Excel formats.

To Export a Table to a Spreadsheet

To save a table in a file in spreadsheet format:

1.   Open the Database window by pressing F11.

2.   Select File ➤ Export from the main menu.

3.   Access asks for the Data Destination. Select the spreadsheet format you want. You can select *Microsoft Excel*, *Lotus (WKS)*, or *Lotus (WK1)*. Access can also import from and export to some other formats that spreadsheets can read, such as delimited text. WKS files are read and written by almost all spreadsheets. Select OK.

4.   Select the name of the table you want to export from the list Access displays, then select OK.

5.   Access displays the Export to File dialog box. Select the drive where you want the spreadsheet file stored from the Drives box. Likewise, select the directory from the Directories box. Enter the file name in the File Name box. (You may also enter the complete file name, including drive and directory, in the File Name box.) Select OK.

6. Access creates a spreadsheet by placing the name of each field in a separate column in the first row of the spreadsheet. Each record is saved as a new row in the spreadsheet.

To Import Data from a Spreadsheet

To import data saved in a spreadsheet into an Access table:

1. Open the Database window by pressing F11.

2. Select File ➤ Import from the main menu.

3. Access asks for the Data Source in the Import box. Select the spreadsheet format you want. You can select *Microsoft Excel, Lotus (WKS), Lotus (WK1),* or *Lotus (WK3).* Select OK.

4. Select from the File Name list the name of the spreadsheet file you want to import . Select the Import button. Access displays the Import Spreadsheet Options dialog box.

5. Check the First Row Contains Field Names box if you want Access to create field names using the values in the first row of the spreadsheet. If you do not check this box, Access creates its own sequentially numbered field names, which you can modify in the table's Design view.

6. Check the Create New Table button if you want Access to create a new table and add the spreadsheet data to it, and go to step 8.

7. Select the Append to Existing Table button to add records from the spreadsheet to an existing table.

- If you select Append to Existing Table, you must select the table name from the pull-down list that follows, and the fields in the spreadsheet must match the data type of the fields in the existing table. The columns in the spreadsheet must be in the same order as the corresponding fields in the table, unless you have checked the First Row Contains Field Names box, in which case the field names in the first row of the spreadsheet must exactly match the field names in the table.

8. To import a portion of the spreadsheet, enter the range of cells in the Spreadsheet Range box.

- If the range has been named, you can enter the named range in the Spreadsheet Range box.

- If you have selected the First Row Contains Field Names option, be sure your range includes the spreadsheet row that contains the field names.

9. Choose OK.

See Also   *Attach a Database File; Export a Table*

SQL DATABASES

SQL stands for *Structured Query Language,* a standardized technique for accessing data stored in a database. SQL is useful for transferring data between programs.

To Attach or Import an SQL Database Table

To attach or import a file from an SQL database:

1. Be sure a Microsoft Access database is open.

2. Select File ➤ Attach Table from the main menu to attach an SQL database file. Select File ➤ Import to import an SQL database file.

3. Select <SQL> Database as the Data Source.

4. Select the ODBC data source you want to use.

5. Enter your login ID and password as used on the SQL database server. Select OK.

6. Select the name of the table you want to attach or import from the Objects list.

7. Select Import or Attach, depending on which action you want to perform.

8. Repeat step 6 to attach another table, if needed. Select Close when you have selected all the necessary tables.

To Export an Access Table to an SQL Database Table

To export a table defined in Access to a table in SQL Database format:

1. Open the Database window by pressing F11.

2. Select File ➤ Export. Access displays an Export dialog box.

3. In the Data Destination area, select <SQL Database>, then select OK.

4. Access shows a list of tables available in the current Access database. Select the one you want to export, then select OK. Access displays an Export dialog box.

5. In the SQL Table box, enter the name of the database you want to create as an SQL table. Select OK.

6. Access displays an SQL Data Sources dialog box. Select the ODBC type you want to export to. Select OK.

7. Enter your login ID and password that you use to login to the SQL database server. Select OK.

8. Access logs in to your SQL database server and exports the Access table to an SQL table. Access displays its progress in a status bar at the bottom of the Access window.

See Also   *Attach a Database File; Export a Table*

SQL STATEMENTS

When you create a query, Access allows you to view the equivalent SQL statements in a special window. You can also modify the SQL statements in this window; your changes will be reflected in the QBE grid when you close the SQL window.

You can also use the SQL statements generated in a query in forms, reports, and macros.

To View and/or Change SQL Statements in a Query

Once you create a query, you can view the equivalent SQL statements and change them this way:

1. With a query in Design view, select View ➤ SQL from the main menu. See *Design View* for more information.

2. Access displays an SQL dialog box, and presents the SQL statement in the SQL Text box, shown in Figure III.24. To make changes, modify the text within the SQL Text box directly. You can add new lines to the text at any time by pressing Ctrl-Enter. To copy, cut and paste, use Ctrl-C, Ctrl-X, and Ctrl-V respectively. The Edit menu does not work when the SQL dialog box is active.

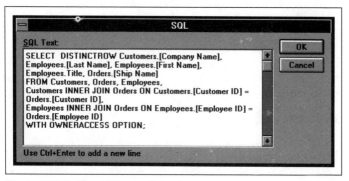

Figure III.24: The SQL text dialog box

3. When you have finished making your changes, select OK. To abandon your changes, select Cancel.

4. If you have made a syntax error in the SQL text box, Access notes the error. Select OK and make the necessary corrections and go to step 3.

5. Access returns you to the Query window. If you selected OK in step 3, your changes are reflected in the QBE grid.

To Use SQL Statements from a Query in a Form, Report, or Macro

You can use an existing query or a new query to establish the conditions (and create the SQL expression) you want to use. The following instructions assume the query exists.

1. With a query in Design view, select View ➤ SQL from the main menu. See *Design View* for more information.

2. Access displays an SQL dialog box, and presents the SQL statement in the SQL Text box. Make any changes as needed.

3. Select the statement using the mouse or keyboard. Press Ctrl-C to copy the text to the Clipboard. Note that you *cannot* select Edit ➤ Copy from the main menu.

4. Choose Cancel.

5. Move to the location where you want the SQL statement to be placed. For example, you can use the statement in a Record Source property of a form or report. Press Ctrl-V or select Edit ➤ Paste from the main menu. Access inserts the text at the new location.

● **WARNING** Access may truncate long SQL statements when you use them in another Access object.

See Also *Queries*

SUBFORMS

See *Forms*

TAB ORDER

By default, Access moves between controls on a form from top to bottom, left to right, when you press Tab.

To Change the Tab Order of a Form

To change the order in which pressing Tab moves to the next control:

1. Open the form in Design view. See *Design View* for more information.

2. Select Edit ➤ Tab Order. Access displays the Tab Order dialog box, shown in Figure III.25, and displays the fields in the current tab order.

3. Select the control you want to move by clicking in the box to the left of the field name and dragging the control to the new location. To move more than one control, select the range of consecutive controls by clicking and dragging over a group, then drag the group to the new location.

4. Select the OK button.

To Restore the Tab Order of a Form

To restore the tab order to moving between fields from left to right, top to bottom on a form:

1. Open the form in Design view. See *Design View* for more information.

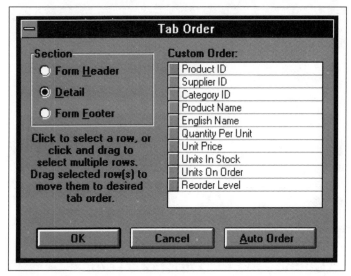

Figure III.25: The Tab Order dialog box

2. Select Edit ➤ Tab Order. Access displays the Tab Order dialog box and displays the fields in the current tab order.

3. Select the Auto Order button.

4. Select OK.

See Also *Forms*

TABLES

Tables are the building blocks of Access. They store the data you want to keep. Each table is divided into records; each record contains information about a single item. In turn, records are divided into fields, the individual units which keep the lowest level of detail.

To Create a Table

To create a new table in Access:

1. Open the Database window by pressing F11.

2. Select the Table button.

3. Select the New button. Access opens the Table window shown in Figure A.2 in the Appendix.

4. Enter the field name in the first column for each field you want to include in the table. Select a Data Type for each field. You can enter a description if you wish; the Description field is optional.

5. Set the properties for each field by using the Field Properties section of the Table window.

6. Set the primary key.

● **TIP** To move the field to a new location, click in the box to the left of the field name, then click and drag the field to the new location.

See Also *Data Types; Fields; Primary Key; Index; Records*

To Save a Table

To save a table in Access:

1. Select File ➤ Save from the main menu.

2. If the table is new and has not been saved, Access asks you to name the table. Enter the table name and select OK.

3. If you have not defined a primary key in the table, Access asks if it should create one for you. If you click on Yes, Access adds a field of data type Counter as the first field in your table.

To Change a Field Property in a Table

To modify the value of a property for a field:

1. Select any cell in the row containing the field you want to change. Use Tab or Shift-Tab to move to the proper row.

2. Select the field property you want to change. You can select a field property in one of two ways:

- Press F6 to move to the Field Properties window, then use ↑ and ↓ to move to the cell next to the property you want to change.
- Click directly in the cell next to the property you want to change.

3. Enter the new value for the property.

4. Click anywhere else on the screen to set the property value.

To View a Table's Design

To examine the contents of a table:

1. Open the Database window by pressing F11. Click on the Table button. Access displays an alphabetical list of the tables in the current database.

2. Highlight the table you want to view. You can use ↑ and ↓ to move the highlight bar to the table name, or click on the table name with the mouse.

3. Select the Design button at the top of the window or double-click on the table name.

Access displays the table you selected. Figure A.2 in the Appendix shows the Table window for a new table.

Each field in the table is defined and described on a separate line in the spreadsheet-like view.

The first column in the table is used to name each field; field names can be up to 64 characters long. The next column specifies the field type, which tells Access the kind of information that can be stored in the field. For example, a text field can store letters and numbers.

The field length is shown or set in the Field Size property setting in the Field Properties box at the bottom of the window.

You can enter a description in the third column of the upper grid. This information is only to remind you of the purpose or content of the field; the text is not used by Access.

Below the table definition window is a Field Properties window. In this section, you specify further details about each field. As you move between fields, the Field Properties change to reflect information about the selected field.

Key fields are unique values you assign to a record. No two records in a database can contain the same value in a key field. In the Employees table shown in Figure A.3 in the Appendix, Employee ID is the key field, indicated by a key symbol at the left edge of the table. Since key fields must be unique and may be tied to other tables in a one-to-many or many-to-many relationship, you cannot change the data type of a key field, and you may not change the value in the key field in any record. Data types can be changed for *non-key* fields.

To View a Table's Data

In Design view, you can modify the fields and their properties in a table. To see the actual *data* in the table, you must change to Datasheet view.

In Datasheet view, Access displays the information stored within records in a *Datasheet*, a grid that resembles a spreadsheet.

To switch to Datasheet view and see the datasheet, click on the Table view button. This is the second button from the left in the tool bar and shows a miniature spreadsheet. Alternatively, you can select View ➤ Datasheet from the main menu.

Access displays the Datasheet view of the table, listing the contents of each field in a column. Columns are arranged in the same order as they are defined. Each record is displayed on a separate line.

To Print a Table

To print records in a table:

1. Open the table in Datasheet view or select the table from the Database window.

2. Select File ➤ Print from the main menu.

3. Select the print options, then select OK.

To print selected records in a table:

1. Open the table in Datasheet view.

2. Select the records you want to print.

- To select a single record, click in the box to the left of the row; the row is displayed in reverse video.

- To select a range of records, click on the first row and drag the mouse to the last row, or click on the first row, then press Shift and select the last row in the range.

- To select all records, choose Edit ➤ Select All records from the main menu.

3. Select File ➤ Print. Access displays a Print dialog box.

4. In the Print Range section choose Selection.

5. Select OK.

See Also   *Datasheets; Printing*

TEMPLATES

When you create a form or report, you can use its characteristics as the basis of new forms or reports. The set of characteristics Access uses, such as the sections used, their height and width, and default fonts, is called a *template*.

You do not need to save a special file in order to create a template: Access reads the characteristics from the form or report you specify as a template using the Form Template procedure. When you design new forms or reports without using the ReportWizard and the Form Template option is set, the characteristics will be automatically applied.

To Set a Form or Report Design as a Template

To tell Access which form or report to use as a template for future forms and reports:

1. Select View ➤ Options from the main menu. Access displays the Options dialog box.

2. Select Form and Report Design from the Category list, shown in Figure III.26.

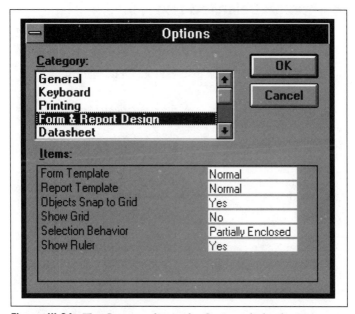

Figure III.26: The Category list in the Options dialog box

3.   In the cell to the right of Form Template, enter the name of the
form you want to use as the template for new forms. In the
cell to the right of Report Template, enter the name of the
report you want to use as the template for new reports.

4.   Select OK.

TEXT FILES

Access can import two types of text files: one in which each field is
delimited by a character (usually a comma), and fixed-width text
files, in which each field in a record begins at the same position relative to the beginning of the record.

To Import a Delimited Text File

To import the data in a delimited text file and use it in an Access
table:

1.   Open a database file that will contain the data in the
delimited text file.

2.   Select File ➤ Import from the main menu. Access displays
the Data Source list box.

3.   Select Text (Delimited) and choose OK. Access displays
a Select File dialog box.

4.   Choose the file you want to import. Select the Import
button. Access displays the Import Text Options dialog
box and displays the name of the text file you selected in
the title of the window.

5.   If the first record in the text file contains the names of the
fields, check the First Row contains a Field Names box.

6. If you want to add the data from your text file to an existing table, select the Append to Existing Table option and enter the table name. Fields must be in the same order as in the receiving table, and data types must be the same in both the imported file and the existing table.

7. Select the Options button; Access opens the window to display option settings. Select the options you want, including the Text Delimiter (the character that separates fields within a record), and date, time, and number options.

8. To use a previous specification, enter the specification name in the Specification Name box. If you want to save your current specifications to use when importing another file, select Save As, enter the file name, and select OK.

9. Select OK in the Import Text Options box. Access creates the table (if requested) and imports the data, displaying its progress in the status bar at the bottom of the window. Select Close.

To Create an Import/Export Specification

In a fixed-width text file, fields in a record are not separated by a character. Instead, each field begins in a specified location (column) relative to the beginning of the file. You must create a specification before you import or export a fixed-width text file.

You may create a specification for a delimited file using the same technique.

To create the specification:

1. Display the Database window by pressing F11.

2. Select File ➤ Imp/Exp Setup from the main menu.

3. To edit an existing specification, enter the name or click on the down-pointing arrow key (or press Alt-↓) and select the specification name from the list Access displays. If you are creating a new specification, leave the Specification Name field empty.

4. If you are creating the specification for a delimited text file, enter the options shown in Text Delimiter and Field Separator boxes. Otherwise, fill in the Field Name, its Data Type, the Starting Column (the first field in a record begins in column 1), and the length of each field in the Field Information section. Figure III.27 shows the Import/Export Setup dialog box.

5. Make your selections in the Dates, Times, and Numbers section.

6. If you are creating a new specification file, select Save As to save the specification.

7. Select OK.

To Import a Fixed-Width Text File

To import a text file in which each field begins at a specified location relative to the first position (column) within a record:

1. Open the database that will contain the records within the text file.

2. Select File ➤ Import from the main menu. Access displays a Data Source list box.

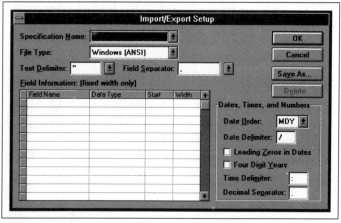

Figure III.27: The Import/Export Setup dialog box

3. Select Text (Fixed Width) and select OK.

4. Select the name of the file you want, then select Import. Access displays the Import Text Options dialog box.

5. If you want to create a new table, be sure the Create New Table option is selected. To add the records from the text file to an existing table, select Append to Existing Table and select the table name.

6. In the Specification Name box, enter the specification name corresponding to the text file you are importing. The specification file contains the field names, data types, positions, and lengths of the fields in the text file.

7. Select OK.

8. Access creates the table (if requested) and imports the data, displaying its progress in the status bar at the bottom of the window. Select Close.

To Export an Access Table to a Text File

Access can export a table to either delimited text or fixed-width text files.

1. Open the Database window by pressing F11.

2. Select File ➤ Export from the main menu.

3. In the Export dialog box select Text (Delimited) or Text (Fixed Width) and select OK.

4. Access displays the list of tables. Select the one you want to export. Select OK.

5. Access displays the Export To File dialog box. Enter the name of the text file you want to create in the File Name box, then select OK.

6. If you selected the Delimited option in step 3, Access asks you if you want to store field names in the first row. Check the box to do so. If you selected the Fixed Width option in step 3, Access asks you to enter the name of the specification. Select OK.

7.   Access exports the table and displays its progress in the status bar at the bottom of the Access window.

See Also   *Attach a Database File; Export a Table*

TOGGLE BUTTONS

See *Option Groups*

TOOL BAR

The tool bar is a set of buttons at the top of the Access window that lets you perform common tasks quickly. The tool bar changes depending on the type of object you are working on and the view you are using. You cannot customize the tool bar in Access.

The inside front and back covers display all the tool bars.

TOOLBOX

Access displays a toolbox in the lower-left corner of the screen when you are in Design view of a form or report. The toolbox lets you select the type of control you want to add to a form or report. To specify the tool, click on it once, then select the field you want bound to the control, and move the pointer to the form or report surface.

The inside front cover illustrates the toolbox.

● **TIP**   To add the same type of control repeatedly, select the type of control, then select the Lock button at the bottom of the toolbox. This locks the control button so that all new controls added to the form or report are the same type. To remove the lock, click on the Lock button again.

UNDO

If you make a mistake or change your mind, you can often undo a change.

To Reverse an Action or Undo a Change

To revert to an early entry or undo an action:

1.   Select Edit from the main menu.

2.   In the drop-down menu list, the first option shows what you can undo. For example, if you are typing new text in a control, Access displays the option Undo Typing. Select the option and Access undoes your work.

3.   If Access displays Can't Undo in the pull-down menu, it cannot reverse your actions.

● **TIP**   When you can undo your work, Access changes the the Undo button in the tool bar from grey to black. The Undo button is the second button from the right on most tool bars (illustrated on the inside covers), and looks like an eraser moving across several stripped lines. To quickly undo your work, click on the Undo button.

UNLINKING TABLES

When you attach tables from another database, the attachment, called a *link*, remains in place, even if the table no longer exists.

To Remove a Link to A Table

To delete an existing link to a table:

1. Open the Database window by pressing F11.
2. Select the Table button.
3. Highlight the table name or click on it with the mouse to select it.
4. Press Del or select Edit ➤ Delete from the main menu.
5. Access removes the link and the table's name from the table list.

See Also   *Attach a Database File; Joining Tables*

USER AND GROUP ACCOUNTS

User accounts are assigned to an individual. Users are then assigned to group accounts. Permissions (the details of what a user can read, edit, or update) are granted to groups (and thus to all the users defined in that group) as well as directly to users.

You can administer security only if your user account name is a member of the group called Admin.

To Add a User Account

To create a new user account in a secured system:

1.   Open the Database window by pressing F11.

2.   Select Security ➤ Users.

3.   Enter the user name in the Name box. User names are *not* case sensitive, can be up to 20 characters long, and may contain letters, numbers, spaces (although the first character *cannot* be a space), and symbols. A user name may not contain any of the following:

"* ? / \ [ ] < > | + = , ; :

Characters between ASCII 00 and 31

4.   Select New. Access displays the New User/Group dialog box.

5.   Access creates a user account code based on the name entered in the Name box plus the four-digit number entered in the Personal ID Number box. Enter the user name or skip the field to accept the name entered in step 3, then select OK.

● **TIP**   Be sure to keep a record of the Personal ID Number. It is needed when you want to share information across more than one computer system.

To Delete a User Account

To erase a user account in a secured system:

1.   Open the Database window by pressing F11.

2.   Select Security ➤ Users.

3.   Enter the user name in the Name box, or select a name from the pull-down list.

4.   Select Delete.

To Use the Special Admin User

Access can restrict the system to authorized users by means of user names and passwords. To administer the security system, your user name must be part of the Admin user group. To set up the security administration of an Access system:

1. Open the Database window by pressing F11.

2. Change the password of the Admin account. When Access is installed, the password for this account is blank. See *Passwords* for instructions on changing a password.

3. Create a new user account for the system administrator. Add the account to the Admin group, which is created when Access is installed. See *To Add a User Account* above for directions on creating a user account.

4. Exit Microsoft Access and restart the program.

5. Log on to Access using the new user name and password set in steps 2 and 3.

6. Delete the Admin user account. See *To Delete a User Account* above for directions.

To Create a User Group

User groups establish the security levels, called permissions, for users assigned to the group. A user can be a member of more than one group.

1. Open the Database window by pressing F11.

2. Select Security ➤ Users.

3. Enter the group name in the Name box. Group names are *not* case sensitive, can be up to 20 characters long, and may contain letters, numbers, spaces (although the first character *cannot* be a space), and symbols. A group name may not contain any of the following:

   " * ? / \ [ ] < > | + = , ; :

   Characters between ASCII 00 and 31

4. Select New. Access displays the New User/Group dialog box.

5. Access creates a group account code based on the name entered in the Name box plus the four-digit number entered in the Personal ID Number box. Enter the group name or skip the field to accept the group name entered in step 3. Select OK.

● **TIP** Be sure to note the Personal ID Number (PIN). If you want to give users access to another computer system that runs Access, you must create the same group name, including the PIN, on the other computer system.

To Delete a User Group

To remove a user group from the Access security system:

1. Select Security ➤ Groups.

2. Enter the group name you want to delete in the Name box, or select the group name from the pull-down list.

3. Select Delete.

To Add a User to a Group

To add an existing user name to a user group:

1. Open the Database window by pressing F11.

2. Select Security ➤ Users from the main menu.

3. In the Users dialog box, enter the user name in the Name box, or select a name from the pull down menu.

4. Select the group you want to add the user to from the Available Groups list.

5. Select Add.

To Remove a User From a Group

To remove a user name from a user group:

1. Open the Database window by pressing F11.

2. Select Security ➤ Users from the main menu.

3. In the Users dialog box, enter the user name in the Name box, or select a name from the pull down menu.

4. Select the group from which the user is to be removed from the Member Of list.

5. Select Remove.

● **SEE ALSO** *Passwords; Permissions*

UNIQUE VALUES

To display only unique values in a select or crosstab query, open the query in Design view, then select View ➤ Query Properties from the main menu. Click in the box to the left of Unique Values Only, or press Alt-U. An *X* appears in the box. Select OK.

VALIDATING DATA

Validation rules allow you to specify when data entered in Access is acceptable. Validation rules put limits on a field or form, such as insisting that a control contain data, be greater than a minimum value, or that two or more fields contain data that is not mutually exclusive.

A validation rule is an expression that tests the data in a control or form. Validation text appears in a window during data entry if the value entered in the field or form does not satisfy the validation rule. For example, if the Validation text is set to *Date entered is not valid* for a date field, the message will pop up in a window if an entry in the date field does not meet pass the validation rule—if the expression in the validation rule property does not evaluate to true.

Access automatically prevents duplicate entries if the field bound to a control is the primary key. You set the primary key by setting the field's Indexed property to Yes (No Duplicates) in a table's Design view.

To Add a Validation Rule to a Control

To add a validation rule and validation text to a control:

1. Open the form in Design view.

2. Select the control.

3. If the Property window is not visible, open it by clicking on the Properties button or selecting View ➤ Properties from the main menu.

4. Enter the expression you want evaluated in the cell to the right of ValidationRule.

5. Enter the text you want displayed automatically by Access if the data entered in the control does not meet the validation criteria in the cell to the right of ValidationText.

Sample Validation Rules

The following examples illustrate the kind of expressions you can enter in the ValidationRule property of a control.

Validation rule	Validation performed
= "Seattle"	Value entered must equal Seattle
Not = "WA"	Value entered must not equal WA
Is Not Null	A value must be entered in the field
In ("WA", "OR", "CA")	Value must be WA, OR, or CA
Not In ("WA", "OR", "CA")	Value cannot be WA, OR, or CA

Validation rule	Validation performed
Between 1 And 10	Value must be greater than or equal to 1 and less than or equal to 10 (that is, 1, 2, 3, 4, 5, 6, 7, 8, 9, or 10)
Between #7/1/94# And #7/31/94#	Date entered must be between July 1, 1994 and July 31, 1994, inclusive
>=Date()	Date entered must be on or after the system's current date
Like "W*"	First letter of value must be a W

See Also   *Expressions*

To Validate Forms or Controls with a Macro

To use a macro to validate a form:

1. Open the form in Design view. See *Design View* for more information.

2. If the Property window is not visible, open it by clicking on the Properties button or selecting View ➤ Properties from the main menu.

3. Click anywhere in the form that is not part of a section. For example, click on the gray area at the bottom of a form. The Property window changes its title to Form.

4. Move to the event in the Property window that you want to assign the macro to. The valid events are listed below.

5. In the event's cell, enter the macro name. If the macro is part of a macro group, enter the macro group name, a period, then the macro name (e.g., **macrogroup.mymacro**).

Event names	When executed
BeforeUpdate	Before saving a new record or control, or before saving changed data in a record or control

Event names	When executed
OnCurrent	Before displaying another record
On Delete	Before deleting the current record
OnExit	Before exiting the current control
OnInsert	Before inserting a new record

WILDCARDS

Wildcards allow you to select records whose fields match a pattern. Wildcards can be used on fields that are of data type Text or Date/Time. For a complete list of wildcard characters, see *Expressions, The Like Operator*.

ZOOM BOX

A zoom box provides additional room for you to enter expressions and property values. To open a Zoom box, press Shift-F2. Enter the text in the box, then select OK to enter the value or Cancel to restore the original text. Figure III.28 shows a zoom box.

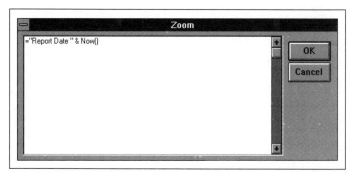

Figure III.28: A zoom box

ZOOM BUTTON

The zoom button on the Printer Preview tool bar (illustrated on the inside back cover) switches between full page view and a close-up view. You cannot set the zoom percentage.

Appendix

Illustrations

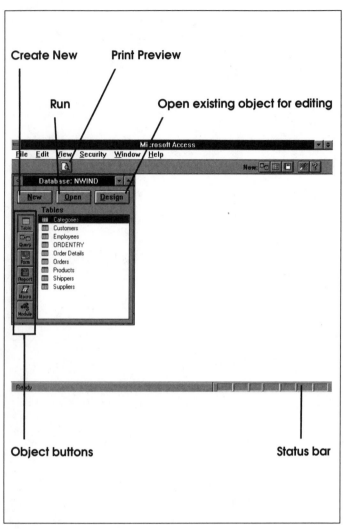

Figure A.1: The Database window

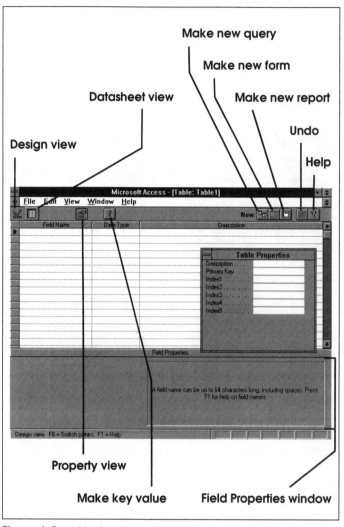

Figure A.2: A blank table in Design view

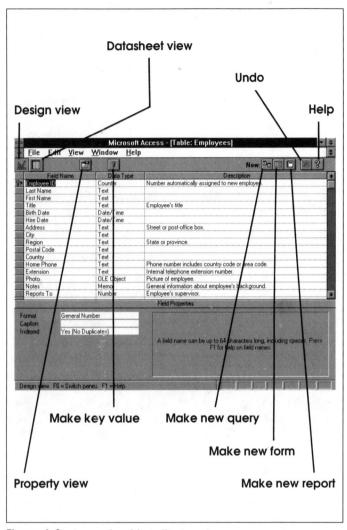

Figure A.3: A sample table in Design view

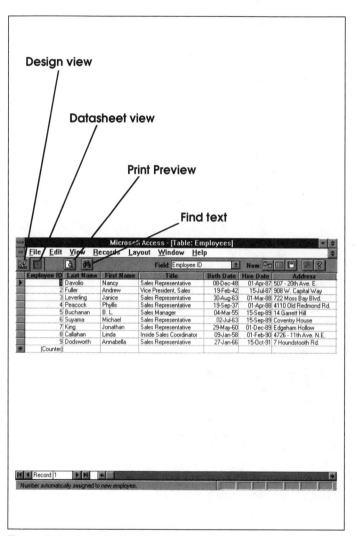

Figure A.4: A sample table in Datasheet view

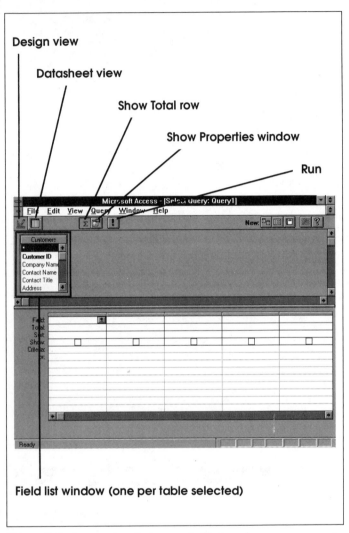

Design view

Datasheet view

Show Total row

Show Properties window

Run

Field list window (one per table selected)

Figure A.5: An empty select query in Design view

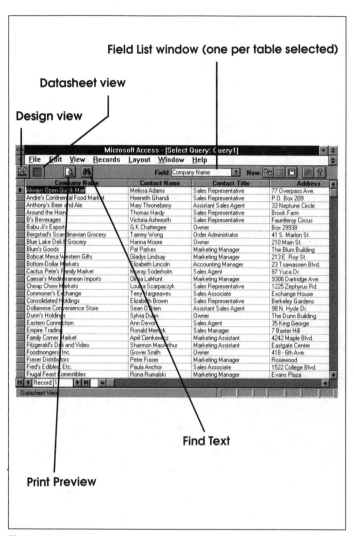

Figure A.6: A sample query in Datasheet view

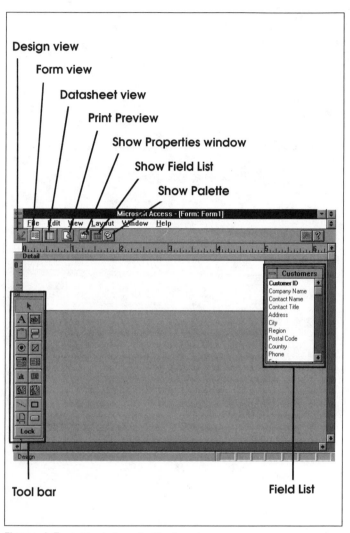

Figure A.7: A blank form in Design view

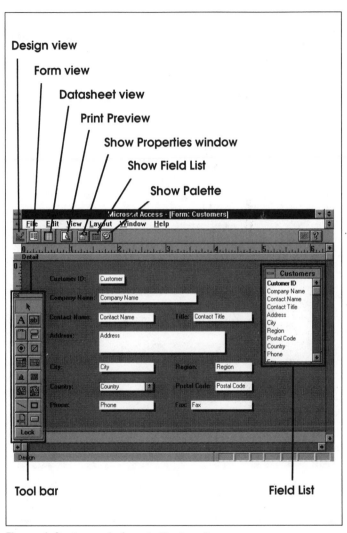

Design view

Form view

Datasheet view

Print Preview

Show Properties window

Show Field List

Show Palette

Tool bar

Field List

Figure A.8: A sample form in Design view

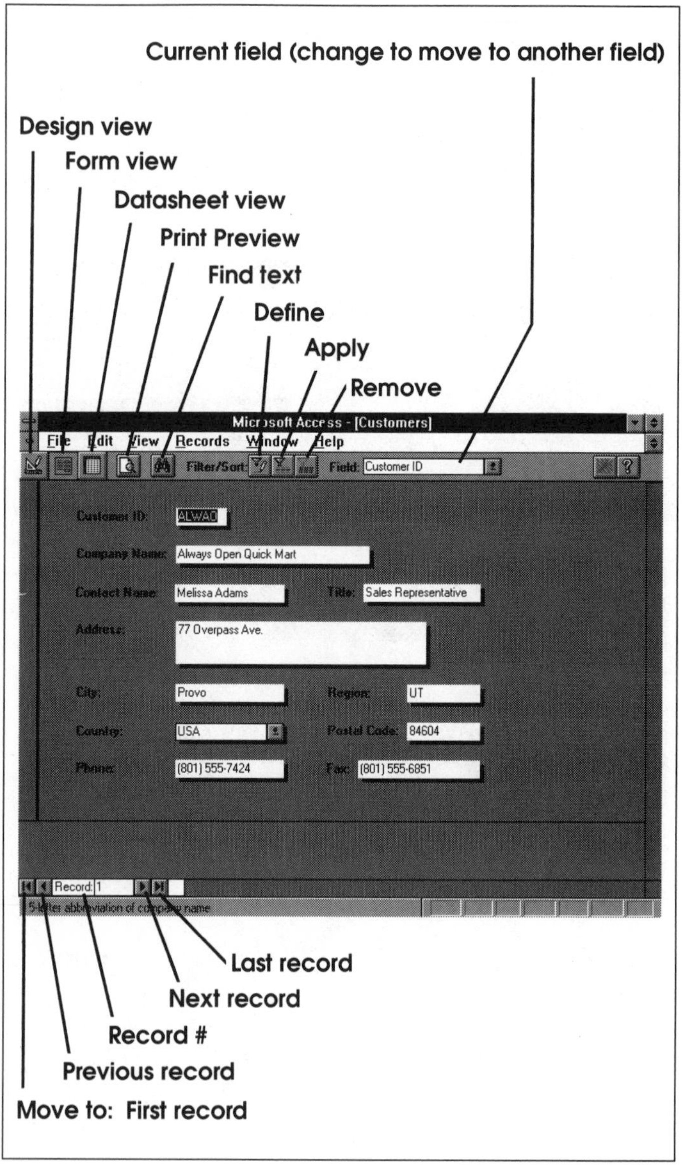

Current field (change to move to another field)

Design view

Form view

Datasheet view

Print Preview

Find text

Define

Apply

Remove

Microsoft Access - [Customers]

File   Edit   View   Records   Window   Help

Filter/Sort: Field: Customer ID

Customer ID:	ALWAO
Company Name:	Always Open Quick Mart
Contact Name:	Melissa Adams	Title:	Sales Representative
Address:	77 Overpass Ave.
City:	Provo	Region:	UT
Country:	USA	Postal Code:	84604
Phone:	(801) 555-7424	Fax:	(801) 555-6851

Record: 1

5-letter abbreviation of company name

Last record

Next record

Record #

Previous record

Move to: First record

Figure A.9: A sample form in Form view

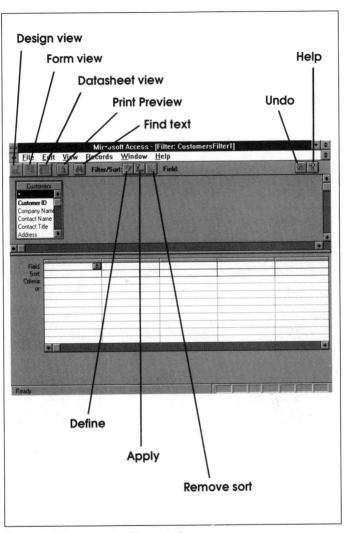

Figure A.10: An empty filter window

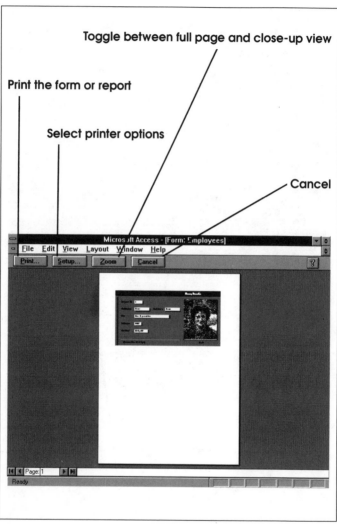

Figure A.11: A form in Print Preview view

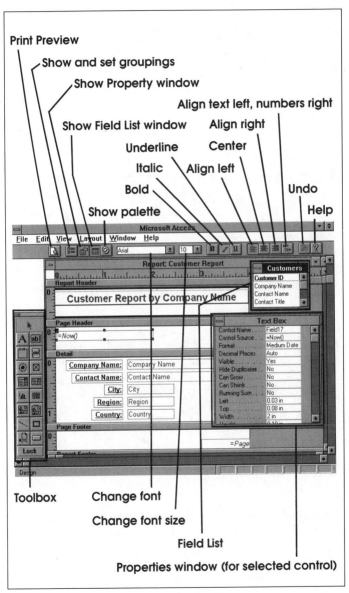

Print Preview

Show and set groupings

Show Property window

Align text left, numbers right

Show Field List window   Align right

Underline   Center

Italic   Align left

Bold   Undo

Show palette   Help

Toolbox

Change font

Change font size

Field List

Properties window (for selected control)

Figure A.12: A sample report in Design view

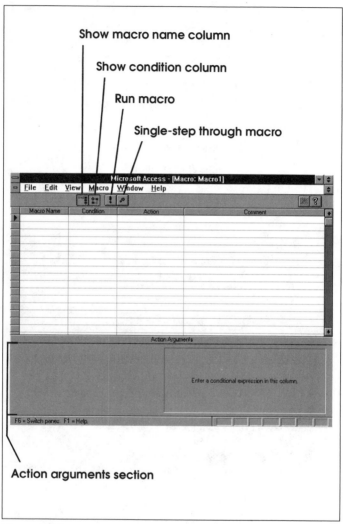

Figure A.13: An empty macro window in Design view

Design view

Datasheet view

Show Total row

Show Properties window

Run

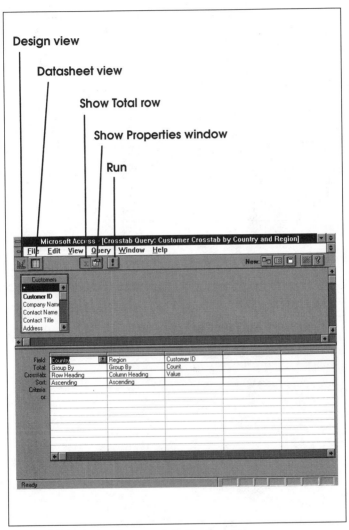

Figure A.14: A sample crosstab in Design view

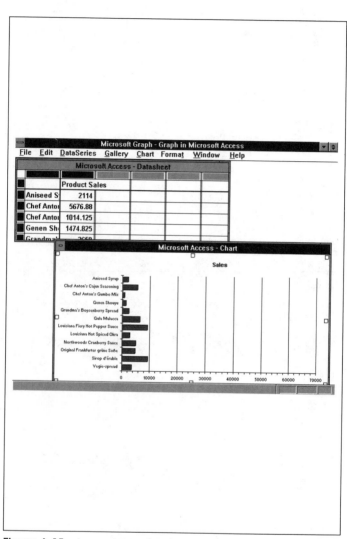

Figure A.15: A sample graph in Design view

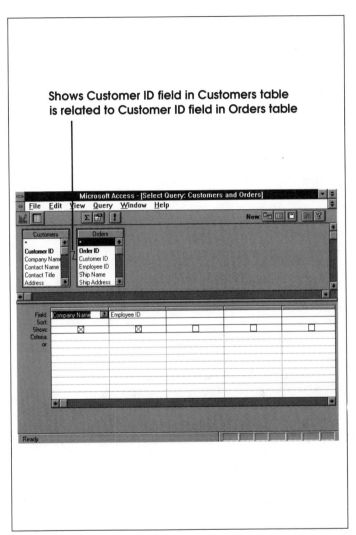

Figure A.16: A query with two joined tables

Index

This index differentiates between *mentions* of items and *explanations* of items. Explanations are listed as **bold** page numbers and mentions as normal text page numbers. Figures are listed as *italic* page numbers.